Selling The Scream

Overheard about Robert Fishbone

"Robert Fishbone is a very inventive guy who, by being himself, has inspired college students and corporate employees to be less fearful of the entrepreneurial route. His message is part lecture, part performance and totally engaging. I have used him to convince MBA students that they can take crazy ideas and make them into successful opportunities."
> Steve Epner, Innovator in Residence and Adjunct Professor of Entrepreneurship, Saint Louis University.

"Robert Fishbone taught me that no idea is too crazy or unworthy of consideration. What I have started to do in my organization is carry around a little notebook so that anytime I have a crazy idea, no matter where I am, I write it down. Every Friday I look at the best idea I had for the week and see what I can do to implement it."
> Justin Lacy, Employment Manager Lumiere Place Casino & Hotels

"As an assistant professor teaching entrepreneurship I've found Robert Fishbone to be an incredible tool for helping to spread entrepreneurship across the campus. Fishbone has found the right blend of art, business, and entertainment to reach students of all ages and from all majors. Based on his crazy idea of selling an inflatable Scream, Fishbone not only built a million dollar business, but now shares his rollercoaster ride as an artist-turned-entrepreneur. Fishbone tells it like it is – the good, the bad, and the ugly. Both traditional students and adult-learners will benefit from time spent with Fishbone."
> Barrett Baebler, Director Entrepreneurship Programs Webster University

"As a business leader and CEO of one of the leading promotional companies in the USA I was always on the "lookout" for ways to motivate and inspire our employees. We had the fortunate opportunity to work with Robert Fishbone during a time of historic chaos and growth. Robert provided a warm and welcoming environment for our employees, engaging their participation in team building and creative workshops. The results were measurable; our people learned to work smarter, trust one another more and think of cre-

ative solutions for complicated business problems. His workshop also taught our employees how to maintain a mindset that will continue forward...concepts that embrace winning attitudes and success. His work definitely enriched our employees on both a professional and personal levels. My advice...Try to utilize Robert's skills because his workshops deliver results you can measure."
        Don Goldman
        CEO, Goldman Promotions

"Robert Fishbone is a master at bringing all of the multiple intelligences alive in a way that enchants an audience. He is a master performer but he is more than that: He is also someone who educates while entertaining, someone who appreciates the richness of life and takes his audience into a different – a far more fun – place. He has worked with my school in opening MI conferences and at assemblies and other presentations, and he always surpasses our already-high expectations."
        Tom Hoerr, Director
        New City School, St. Louis

Selling the Scream
Tips and Steps to Becoming a Successful
Entrepreneur With YOUR Crazy Idea
by Robert Fishbone

©2009, ON THE WALL PRODUCTIONS, INC.

First Edition
Printed in the United States of America

Cover and Interior Book Design by Jackie Lynch
www.DesignSharkStudios.com

Cover Photo by Keeven Photography
St. Louis, MO

Book edited by Joyce Cheney
www.FocusCommunications.us

ISBN 13: 978-0-9822999-7-5

ON THE WALL PRODUCTIONS, Inc.
9441 Old Bonhomme Road · Saint Louis, MO 63132

314-692-2900

scream@robertfishbone.com
www.robertfishbone.com

Selling The Scream

Tips and Steps to Becoming a Successful Entrepreneur With YOUR Crazy Idea

By Robert Fishbone

Acknowledgements

Thanks to my wife, best friend and life partner, who is all wonderfully the same person, the splendiferous master scenic artist Sarah Linquist, without whose faith, love and nearly-endless patience this book would not be...

Thanks to our kids, Liza and Tyler, for keeping me on my toes, and finally realizing I do more than just send faxes...

Thanks to my mentors:

Henry and Shirley Fishbone, my parents, who taught me to dance

Dr Alan Toub, my scoutmaster, who challenged me to lead and explore

Mrs. McCallamont, my 12th grade English teacher who insisted I go to Antioch College

Cal Sparks, Bob Divine & Michael Fajans, who inspired me to be my own kind of artist

Babatunde Olatunji, my drumming teacher who gave me the unexpected gift of the bell

Brother Blue, Storyteller, who encouraged me to 'take it on the road'

Bobby Dawson, who helped me get my Scream business off the ground

Phil Myers, who showed me I could do my business on my own

Arthur Scharff, who helped me understand my business so I could eventually sell it

Members of the National Speakers Association for showing me a new path

Thanks to:

Joyce Cheney, my editor, for uncovering a useful book out of my ramblings

Jackie Lynch, for crafting a great overall design

Eric, Kate, Ann, Sue, Jean, Debbie, Leslie, Scott, Shep, Barret, Steve, Remo, Don, Dann, Luis and Joe Kang for extra support all along

My huge circle of encouraging family and friends, and,

Thanks to the Universe for keeping it all so mysterious...

Table of Contents

1. This book: What's in it for you?

Do you have *crazy ideas* you want to get out into the marketplace? Maybe like me, you've come up with a new product. Maybe you want to provide a service. Or maybe you want to innovate within your current workplace.

You're an **entrepreneur**.

Entrepreneurs are people who see opportunities. We have the guts and passion to start new ventures and achieve greater success within our own companies. We become so excited with our visions that we can't sleep at night. There is nothing else like it and there is no better time to begin than right now!

I became an entrepreneur and turned my *crazy idea* into a million dollar business. This book shows how *you* can succeed as well.

And the book will help shape your vision and avoid mistakes I made while turning my *crazy idea* into a financial success! As an artist with no business experience, I learned the ropes one mistake after another and still managed to create a company known around the world for great selling, unusual products and excellent customer service.

My success formula? Perseverence plus creative solutions when problems came up. You can succeed the same way.

My first *crazy idea* was for a "gift product" – an inflatable of a screaming guy, inspired by **Edvard Munch**'s famous painting, *"The Scream."* That single item grew into a global company selling over 150 art-inspired projects in over 20 countries.

If your *crazy idea* is a product, you can follow the steps in this book to success.

Or maybe you're crazy about a something else – a new service, a web venture or even an innovation within the company you currently work for or own. This book's step-by-step approach will work for your *crazy idea*, too.

My business launched in the days before the Internet, so you'll do some tasks differently now, but the same entrepreneurial steps and skills apply:

- Fall in love with your *crazy idea*.
- Embrace risk taking as a means to continual innovation, but be prudent, too.
- Evaluate your idea.
- Identify your niche in the marketplace.
- Make a plan and stick to it.
- Solve problems creatively.
- Identify resources.
- Get help.

You can do this: *you're a creative thinker, an entrepreneur!*

This book gives you proven success tools:

- Three Power Affirmations
- Five Success Secrets
- 81 Fishtips™
- 155 Action Steps
- 50 Resources
- 89 **Glossary Terms**

These tools will help you speed right along on your roller coaster ride of entrepreneurial success. As you read this book, keep a yellow pad next to you and write out your own scenario as mine unfolds. Use my story and action steps as a blueprint for your own plan. **REALLY DO IT.** You've already got at least one *crazy idea* floating around in your brain....

If you do follow the advice right here, you'll end up knowing the direction to take – and you'll know how to get there.

It doesn't matter if you are an artist or a bean counter; it doesn't matter if you have an idea for a product or a service or a new twist for your current workplace. By having confidence in yourself, by valuing your dream, and by finding the right assistance, you too can make your own *crazy idea* a reality.

Selling The Scream

Sound good? Ready? Let's Get Started!

Take Action

▶ Read my story. (OK, laugh at my mistakes if you want.)
▶ Use the tools in this book:
    DO the Action Steps
    SAY the Affirmations
    USE the Fishtips™, Success Secrets and Resources
▶ There's one more requirement: Have fun!

"Confidence can get you where you want to go, and getting there is a daily process. It's so much easier when you feel good about yourself, your abilities and talents."

Donald Trump
Real Estate Developer and
TV Personality

"The way to get started is to quit talking and begin doing."

Walt Disney
Animator, Entrepreneur
and Philanthropist

Selling The Scream

So you've got a *crazy idea*...

Selling The Scream

2. *CRAZY IDEA* or just *CRAZY*?

 Fishtip™: Don't let the craziness of your *crazy idea* stop you: *let it inspire you.*

Ideas. We all have them rambling through our brains. Good, bad, monumental, silly, forbidden, improbable, and my personal favorite, *crazy*. The journey begins with "I wonder if..."

This book tells the story of my *crazy idea*. I was so passionate about it that I convinced my wife, after much discussion, to risk our life savings to give my scheme a try. Looking back though, it is amazing that we went through with it.

You already know that the road to success is tough, with forces and events that will hold you back, pull you off course, and sabotage your best-laid plans. "You can't do that...it's crazy!" I couldn't pass up that challenge. You?

Whether it is a small improvement or an earth shaking innovation I hope that my own improbable journey inspires and gives you the confidence and practical tools to make *your crazy idea* succeed.

> *"Do something. If it doesn't work, do something else. No idea is too crazy."*
>
> Jim Hightower
> *Syndicated Columnist, Author*

Selling The Scream

3. What's your dream?

 Fishtip™: Cast caution to the wind...*what is your heart's desire?*

You don't just want another job, do you? You're inspired; you want to reach for your dream:

- Create something amazing just to see it take shape: "Check this out!" Manifest your vision, this is what artists do.
- Save or fix the world, "OK, it's working now."
- Make money.

At the beginning, it's all fun! New, exciting, revealing, adventure-some. You see the fulfillment of your desires, maybe:

- Working on your own
- Spending time with family and friends
- Achieving financial freedom
- Helping others

Envision your success. Imagine yourself having achieved your goal, whatever that is. Having the seed of success planted deeply in your brain will do wonders to keep you going.

> *"Formulate and stamp indelibly on your mind a mental picture of yourself as succeeding. Hold this picture tenaciously. Never permit it to fade. Your mind will seek to develop the picture."*
> Norman Vincent Peale
> *Author, The Power of Positive Thinking*

Once you have a goal, having a map, a business plan, will greatly improve your chances of achieving your dream. It will remind you to do what is necessary and NOT DO what is NOT necessary.

If your dream is not happening in your current circumstances, then you have to choose...change your dream to fit your life, give up on your dream, or change your life to fit your dream. The last choice is often how entrepreneurs are born: we deliberately journey into the unknown.

If you take that route, you're in for an exciting trip with lots of up-hills and descents, blind curves, confusing intersections, spectacular views. To sustain you on the journey, you'll need fuel: the following affirmations have really worked for me. No kidding. Say them to yourself every day. Put them on your bathroom mirror, your laptop and your dashboard. On days when you don't quite believe the affirmations, say them anyway and act accordingly.

Three *CRAZY* Affirmations that *Really Work*:

- I have *crazy ideas*.
- I can do this.
- People will help me.

Take Action

▶ Post my proven affirmations and repeat them daily, out loud, with conviction. Put them on a mirror and watch yourself say them.

▶ Craft your own affirmations. Use them.

4. The Power of Yes!

 Fishtip™: You can do it. Believe it and live accordingly.

Antioch College in Yellow Springs, Ohio was my alma mater. People either say, "Antioch? Never heard of it," or, "Oh, you went to Antioch…that explains everything."

Antioch had a well-deserved reputation for attracting and producing liberal, radical, edgy thinkers and doers. The school did everything it could to push us out of our comfort zones and into unexplored territories and to do something new there. Antioch encouraged us to ask, "What else? What if? Why not?"

The school ran a groundbreaking Co-op Program. Every few months, after meeting with advisors and selecting from a wide range of opportunities, students would be plopped down in an unfamiliar, giant city or small town and have to make a life for ourselves: find a place to live, find roommates, get to and from work, pay utilities, share meals…and succeed at our jobs. All the time paying attention to our feelings and experimenting with whether or not we wanted to make this kind of work into a career.

We students quickly learned to marshal our resources to not just survive, but thrive and make use of what the area had to offer. No matter the work experience we learned a lot. And what we especially learned both on campus and out in the world was *The Power of Yes!*

Antioch reinforced the fact that you can do anything, accomplish anything that you want to. Start with a positive attitude. Then ask the right questions of the right people, stay away from nay-sayers, and keep at it!

Make "Anything is possible" the theme of your life, and create a world around you that will support your success. Hang with positive people who encourage you to do the crazy things that are popping up in your mind and out of your mouth…people who say, "Sounds great! You can do it! Can I help?"

Be open to receiving gifts and unexpected offerings. This means that if you are locked into exactly what success means for you, and exactly how to get there, you may miss out on the valuable opportunities made available free of charge from the sidelines. It's those little offhand comments and suggestions that you overhear that will initiate the AHA! moment that will lead to your goal. When you are ready to make things happen, those gifts and offerings will come…

> *"Opportunity dances with those who are ready on the dance floor."*
>
> H. Jackson Browne Jr.
> *Author*

> *"Be ready when opportunity comes. Luck is the time when preparation and opportunity meet."*
>
> Pierre Elliott Trudeau
>
> *Former Canadian Prime Minister*

Take Action!

- ▶ List positive people in your personal and professional life. Who will be your cheerleaders as you pursue your idea? Get them to send you postcards of encouragement. Send postcards to yourself.

- ▶ List the nay-sayers. How can you minimize their influence on you?

- ▶ What are you thankful for?

- ▶ What gifts has the universe given you?

- ▶ Describe specific times in your life when your positive (or negative) attitude has influenced how things came to pass.

Secret #1

The Power of Yes!

Take Action!

▶ Think positive. It really helps. If you don't believe in "The Power of Yes!" yet, act as if you do and see what happens.

▶ You can do it. Believe it and live accordingly.

Selling The Scream

5. Can you really make something out of nothing?

 Fishtip™: The perfect place to start…is where you are right now. *Just take the first step.*

After graduation, my future (and current) wife and I took *The Power of Yes!* with us to St. Louis and it proved to be a life saver.

We had moved there to help start a Community Access Media Center. Our contact was sure he would get a grant to hire us since we had experience with an emerging and promising new medium – portable video equipment.

But the grant fell through and there we were, waiting tables and playing music to make rent. But hey, we full of idealistic, artistic zeal: we were invincible. Except on the days when we had to push start our green VW bug, Otto the Auto, to make it to an appointment; or the time the dash board burst into flames while we were heading to a meeting….really!

We hung on, though. In fact it was on another car ride, delivering newspapers, that we finally saw an opportunity to improve our life. A member of the City Beautification Commission wanted to see more **murals** painted in St. Louis. Though we had never done public art ourselves, we did have friends at college who had created amazing murals. Sarah had an arts background and was a painter, I had experience in understanding systems, fixing things and being naïve, so naturally we both assumed we could do anything, especially monumental projects. Summoning *The Power of Yes!* we looked at each other and said in unison, "Hey, we could do that!" We've repeated that phrase many times over the years. And that is how our career as mural painters began.

We were not afraid of having no direct experience, we weren't worried about how the heck do you do this, so we felt fine about walking into a corporate office to convince the CEO to let us at his wall. We just stayed positive and excited and gathered up everyone and everything we needed and in two months created a striking and huge design – 125 ft. long by five stories tall – and painted it on a prominent wall downtown: a butterfly emerging from a cocoon, in four panels. We made the painting process a continuous happening with dance music blasting and seats for people to hang out, watch, and comment on the art.

The mural and the happening commanded attention and earned rave reviews, great publicity and even our first fan mail. It was a life-affirming experience, and gave us the confidence to move forward.

Our positive attitude and our ability to think fast enabled us to turn that one-time project into a 35-year long run that took us all over the country. We worked for major companies like Monsanto and Southwestern Bell, and for small businesses only the locals have heard of. Our sponsors ranged from huge cultural organizations like the 1982 World's Fair, the National Endowment for the Arts and several states' Arts Councils to neighborhood schools, shops, theatres and even individual families. We painted on everything from ten story buildings to boarded-up windows.

Our work is documented in several books and is housed, via writings and thousands of slides, at the Missouri Historical Society (see Resources). That MHS collection is highly valued as a unique document illustrating urban transformation. Not bad for a couple of artists delivering newspapers and having the confidence to say, "Hey, we could do that!"

Take Action!

▶ Pick up today's newspaper and look for something new being done/built. Imagine that you had the same skills and expertise to make it happen. How would you feel?

▶ Say out loud, "Hey I can do this!"

▶ Go to a big home improvement store, department store or toy store. Walk up and down the aisles. Look at all the stuff. Almost everything there was made by somebody having a *crazy idea* and then saying "Hey, I can do this!" Impressive, huh? Imagine seeing your *crazy idea* on one of the shelves.

> *"Whenever you see a successful business, someone made a courageous decision."*
>
> Peter Drucker
> *Writer, management consultant, and self-described "social ecologist"*

> *"Courage is being scared to death - but saddling up anyway."*
>
> John Wayne
> *Actor*

> *"All you need in this life is ignorance and confidence; then success is sure."*
>
> Mark Twain
> *Author and Humorist*

Selling The Scream

6. You got a problem with that?

 Fishtip™: See problems as challenges. *Solve them creatively.*

My goal for public art and the theme for my current entrepreneurial creativity, is to surprise people, to interrupt their routines with new experiences, thoughts and feelings. To create those catalysts for "wake ups," our murals combined the real and surreal, the beautiful and funny. Our murals started with familiar elements that people could relate to…and invited viewers to step through doors and explore new and different worlds.

People loved those murals! Locals visited their favorites and organized bicycle tours of our work. Bus drivers diverted from their routes to show off the newest murals.

It was also important to us that the people living or working in the area of the artwork felt a sense of ownership of it. We engaged people in the neighborhood during both the design process and the painting and made sure that some elements of the design were things that mattered to them. We painted murals full time. It was hard, very rewarding work.

More than painters though, we saw ourselves, as many artists do, as problem solvers. If you ask most people, "What do artists do?" they will say things like, "Paint, sculpt, dance, act, sing, weave and so on." Those answer "how." But what artists *do* is translate our experience into new forms and share that discovery with others. We look at the world with fresh eyes and ears, assuming that rules are to be broken, that mistakes are opportunities for creative solutions that boldly go where no one has gone before. Innovation is the challenge – and the payoff.

After 18 years, new mural clients called regularly and life was sweet. We worked when we wanted to, traveled when the spirit moved us, and swapped sparks with others in St. Louis' vibrant arts community. And then life got sweeter, and more complicated:

Daily News

Artist Couple Has Kids, Needs More Money; Lots, FAST!

How could we increase our income – without having to get a real job? My intuition said that there was something we already did that I could stretch, bend or shake, rattle and roll into a lucrative new income.

Take Action!

▶ When has a life event changed everything for you?
  How did you handle it?

▶ Are you facing a big change right now?
  How are you handling it?

7. Is it time for a tweak?

 Fishtip™: Before you completely change directions, explore simply adjusting your current course.

A couple of weeks later, up on a ladder, in the midst of a mural, I had a revelation. It didn't come with a loud, booming voice and a cinematic sunset. I just realized something.

We were really good designers. Our murals had become local landmarks and tourist destinations, and were continually featured on TV and in print. I was hired to lecture about murals as transformative forces. As artists-in-residence, we helped students from NYC to Anchorage create permanent murals for their schools. We were rock stars!

People enjoyed our work over and over for free: that expansive enjoyment and experience is the wonderful nature of public art. But there was a flaw in the formula, because we, the painterly rock stars, only got paid once!

We didn't want to grow the company by looking for and accepting more mural jobs, which would have also meant hiring and managing more people. Plus, we were ready for something new. So how could we otherwise multiply ourselves, our talents? Maybe we could create something once and (revised formula!) *get paid* over and over again. We could make multiples…but of what?

Take Action!

▶ What's going pretty well in your life, if only….? What's the flaw in your current formula? What can you do to fix things?

▶ Consider multiples: cottage industries start this way. Did you ever make anything as a one-time project that you thought others might want to have? Or has anyone ever said of something you did or made, "I think a lot of people would want that"? How can you multiply your product? Did you ever feel that there wasn't enough time in the day, or wish that there were more of you to carry out your plans exactly as you want them done? How can you multiply yourself and create a service? Within a company, you can multiply yourself by getting others to think more innovatively. How can you motivate them to bring it up a notch?

> *"Ideas are like rabbits. You get a couple and learn how to handle them, and pretty soon you have a dozen."*
>
> John Steinbeck
> *Author*

> *"To invent, you need a good imagination and a pile of junk."*
>
> Thomas Edison
> *Inventor*

Secret #2

Inspiration is everywhere.

Take Action!

▶ What grabs you? Where do you get your ideas?

▶ How can you get more of whatever that is in your life?

▶ Identify an artist or craftsperson or someone whose work or personal energy you admire and take them to lunch. Ask them what inspires them and where they get their ideas. Try those things yourself.

Selling The Scream

8. AHA!

 Fishtip™: AHA! moments are often simple and obvious in hindsight, but you have to be paying attention to notice them.

"OK, time to **brainstorm**." I started making lists of things I could duplicate and sell. But after all the ideas, inside and outside of my "art world" comfort zone, I came back to murals. Maybe we could do instant murals that people could put up and paint by themselves. Or maybe instead of an actual mural, we could sell finished figures cut out of some material that people could just put up on their walls, even take with them when they moved. We could create them in our workshop and ship them to customers.

This was actually not a totally new idea for us. We had already made several large, one-of-a-kind **cut-out** figures. Mostly, we used cut-outs based on famous paintings to demonstrate our abilities to potential clients. Occasionally, clients commissioned cut-outs of local characters for signs or special events..

Visitors to our office were blown away by eight-foot tall cut-outs of Picasso nudes, Gauguin's Tahitian women, the figure in Munch's *"The Scream"*…. Our *Scream* drew the most comments, by far. "Now that is really weird." For me, Weird = Great, *crazy idea*!

Why not mass-produce giant *Scream* cut-outs and market them to therapists? Imagine: The patient walks into the waiting room, and sees this tortured soul. "OK, I'm feeling pretty good today, way better than that guy. I'm CURED!" We'd get written up in medical journals, do talk shows, make a fortune, and retire! But would enough therapists buy the things? Probably not.

Then I heard about an Edvard Munch exhibit coming to Kansas City's art museum. Hey! We could sell - or rent - the museum some *Scream* cut-outs and they could place them at the airport and in lobbies and stores all over town for publicity. I polished my brilliant pitch on the drive to Kansas City. But when I described my idea to them they reacted like I was speaking Klingon through a kazoo. Silence and head scratching. Then glances amongst them: "Maybe he'll leave soon so we won't have to call security."

I could see that they didn't get it and weren't going to. I left the hallowed halls and drove home, thinking: *There had to be a way.*

The next day, I cruised the St. Louis Art Museum's gift shop and noticed that their selection of art inspired gifts stretched far beyond the usual postcards and posters. Small, start-up companies were beginning to adapt famous artworks onto mugs, hats, t-shirts, umbrellas, fridge magnets, light switch plates, et al. Clearly there was a new market growing for this expanding product category: I was on the right path.

I checked out a **Nature Company** store. Amongst nature note cards and wildlife-sounds CDs, stood a life sized, inflatable penguin. "Cool," I said out loud, to the penguin. "I wonder if we could make an inflatable of the guy in *The Scream*". The AHA! was as simple as that. It usually is.

The Nature Company refused to share their manufacturers' information with me. Then I remembered a past mural client, Acme Premium Supply Company in St. Louis. Acme does product development and sourcing in Asia, and had offered to help us if we ever had a *crazy idea* for a something new. I called Acme, and the short of it? Our inflatable *Scream* is still popular after 18 years and over 500,000 units sold...how about that!

Take Action!

▶ Pay attention to things that grab your attention, and ideas that float thru your brain. Take notes; your cell phone probably has a memo recorder and a camera...use it.

▶ What have you already done that could be modified into a new product or service?

▶ Save names and contact information. Write down why they're meaningful to you, so when you look at that business card in six years, you'll remember. Be nice to everybody. You never know.

▶ Who do you know already who can help you?

9. Are you nuts?

 Fishtip™: Take your *crazy ideas* seriously. Well, some of them anyway.

 Fishtip™: Fall in love with your *crazy idea*. Then evaluate it – by yourself and with your principal advisor.

 Fishtip™: You don't have a principal advisor? Get one NOW!

A few days later, after my conversation with the penguin, I had a conversation with my wife during breakfast.

Hey honey, guess what?

> *What?*

I've got a **crazy Idea**.

> *(Oh no, not again)…that's nice.*

Well, aren't you going to ask me what it is?

> *Ohhh kaaay, what is it?*

I'm going to make something and sell it.

> *Um…Do you have any more of a plan?*

A what?

> *A plan, like a business plan, that shows the various steps you'll follow to accomplish your goals, which you can also use to measure the results, and then make adjustments and modifications along the way to align with how things actually develop, thus making success more likely.*

Hey, I'm not stupid. I know what a business plan is. Anyway, I told you my plan: I'm going to make something and sell it.

> *Where are you going to make it?*

Oh, there are factories all over the place. I'll find one.

How are you going to pay for this?

You know that **CD** we have.

You mean our life savings?

Yeah. You need to spend money if you wanna make money.

Aren't you going to need help?

Oh, I can do it all myself. Besides, when the kids get a little older they can help; we'll get to bond.

Who's going to buy it?

Everybody. We'll get amazing publicity. I'll send it to People Magazine…

Ohhh kaaay…but what about manufacturing quality control, importation, customs and duties, warehousing, client management, office space, data management and back up, shipping options, accounting, a marketing strategy, a sales force, intellectual property protection, expanding the line, finding employees, employee benefits, employee vacations, employee birthday gifts, employee…

Staaaaaaaaahp! Now you're taking all the fun out of it…it's starting to sound like a, a biz-ness…

Well, yeah!

Yeah, well…I'm not going to let you take the wind out of my sails. Pretty soon you'll see my irresistible products in every store and every catalog and we'll sell tons and tons of them and make tons and ton of money….

OK buster, but the proof is in the pudding.

> **"To accomplish great things, we must dream as well as act."**
> Anatole France
> *French poet, journalist and novelist*

Take Action!

▶ Think of 2-3 *crazy ideas* you've had before – and carried thru. For each idea, how'd that go? If things worked out well, what were the keys to that success? If things didn't go well, how come? What could you have done differently?

▶ What *crazy ideas* have you thrown out? Are any worth resurrecting?

▶ What's your new *crazy idea*?

▶ Fall in love with your favorite *crazy idea*. Work with that idea until you're so crazy in love with it that no matter how many people say no, you still believe. Then evaluate it by yourself (see below). Then evaluate it with your principal advisor. Do a reality check: is it really worth pursuing, or are you just insane?

▶ Write down your *crazy idea*. Now evaluate it. Consider:
  ◉ Are you in love with it?
  ◉ Has anyone else ever done it?
  ◉ Were/are they successful?
  ◉ How is your idea different? Why is yours better?
  ◉ Who might buy it?
  ◉ Do you have help?
  ◉ Who can you get to help you do a reality check?
  ◉ Will you be doing something else at the same time, like your current job?
  ◉ How will you make time for your new venture?
  ◉ Do you have a business plan with a timetable? (See What's a business plan anyway?)

> *"Ideas won't keep: something must be done about them."*
>
> **Alfred North Whitehead**
> *English mathematician*
> *and philosopher*

Selling The Scream

Getting Started

☑ *Crazy idea*

☑ Winning attitude

Now how do you make
that *crazy idea* happen?

Selling The Scream

10. Got any experience?

 Fishtip™: You've been an entrepreneur before. Just carry that experience and confidence forward.

It was time to show my wife, and I guess myself, that I really could make money with my *crazy idea*.

But wait! I was just a guy, an artist. What qualifications did I have to be in business, to be an entrepreneur? I searched my past for anything I'd already done that might have prepared me for this new venture.

Most of us did something to earn money when we were young: lawn mowing, a paper route, babysitting, a lemonade stand...I sold eggs. My dad was in the poultry business, and when I was 15, I inherited a sales route from my big brother. Regular customers bought one, two or even three dozen eggs a week. April was the big bonanza, with Easter and Passover being my **Q4**: besides the regular orders, two customers each bought 12 dozen eggs. At thirty cents profit per dozen, plus tips, I made about $10.00 from those two customers alone...big money in 1966. I wanted to earn enough for a trip from New Jersey to Philmont Boy Scout Camp in New Mexico...and I am proud to say that I succeeded!

We never would have thought about it as kids, but in our childhood jobs were the seeds of entrepreneurialism:
- Identifying a need
- Drafting an innovative solution
- Making it happen

As kids, we learned we were capable of running a business. Later on, when it was time to bring our "grown-up" innovations to life, we remembered, "Oh yeah, I did this before. I already know how." Same process, different scale.

Being an egg entrepreneur fit right into "The American Dream." Our young country's history and culture have been defined by entrepreneurship: opportunities for many individuals, plus a spirit of invention. Did you enjoy assembling things when you were a kid? That Thomas Edison, George Washington Carver and **Hedy Lamarr** spirit of invention has defined much of American history and culture, and it helped me get my first wheels. I scrounged some miscellaneous parts and built a delivery bike with a big basket on the front.

That basket could hold six dozen eggs. One day, while delivering eggs to a new customer in a new neighborhood, I rode up on the sidewalk. Since I was unfamiliar with that part of town, I was searching for addresses and didn't notice that one section of the slate sidewalk jutted up over a huge sycamore tree root…we connected.

Slow motion. Like in a dream, four full egg cartons slowly rise from the basket, heading upward into the sun. At the top of their arc, the cartons open and 48 eggs fly into the air. I am surrounded by an egg storm. I am powerless. The eggs float. Finally, after forever, the eggs careen toward the sidewalk. Staccato rhythms of fragile shells meeting stone.

#@$%! Not only do I have to clean everything up, but I lose my initial investment, my profit and my tip. I lose the time it takes to clean up the mess and the time and money it takes to deliver more eggs. What can I do to keep this from ever happening again?

This is entrepreneurial thinking.

Innovation doesn't have to be complex, just new. Here's an example: Russian and US astronauts all used regular pencils in space. They were worried that the graphite would break off, float around, get jammed in equipment, and cause big problems. The urban legend goes… that NASA spent millions developing a pen that would write in space; actually it was American Paul Fisher who invested over a million dollars of his own money developing the space pen. It's been said that Russian cosmonauts simply started using grease pencils.

My solution for egg transport was simply to stretch rubber bands across the top of the basket.

Take Action!

▶ When have you been an entrepreneur before? If you succeeded, what made it work? If not, how come? What can you do differently now? You're probably not going to sell lemonade or mow lawns this time, but what can you learn from that prior experience?

▶ See www.lemonadeday.org in Resources

"I'm not sure I knew what an entrepreneur was when I was ten, but I knew that starting little businesses and trying to sell greeting cards or newspapers door-to-door... there's just something very intriguing to me about that."

Steve Case
CO-Founder of America Online

"The entrepreneur is our visionary, the creator in each of us. We're born with that quality and it defines our lives as we respond to what we see, hear, feel, and experience. It is developed, nurtured, and given space to flourish or is squelched, thwarted, without air or stimulation, and dies."

Michael Gerber
Author and entrepreneur

So like, what kind of business do you want, or need to be?

Here are brief descriptions of common business entities you should investigate before going too far in establishing your operations; there are others as well. Differences involve responsibility, liability and distribution of profits. Get advice from a mentor, lawyer and accountant before deciding.

Sole proprietorship: Refers to an individual doing business in their own name and in which there is only one owner. They may do business with a trade name other than their legal name, hence the term, dba, Doing Business As.

Simple Partnership: In a SP, each partner makes an equal contribution of time, effort and capital; they share equally in the losses and profits, and in decision making. Often, a partnership is formed among persons who contribute different kinds of expertise.

Limited Liability Partnership (LLP) is a partnership in which some or all partners have limited liability. It therefore exhibits elements of partnerships and corporations. It is often made up of professionals and helps to shield innocent members of the partnership from liability.

Corporation: A corporation is a legal entity separate from the persons that form it. Besides officers, there are shareholders and a board of directors. If a corporation fails, shareholders normally only stand to lose their investment and are not held personally liable. It can be formed by one or more people.

Not for profit: the non-profit corporation exists solely to provide programs and services of public benefit.

11. What's a business plan anyway?

 Fishtip™: Make a business plan, even a simple one, and stick to it.

Yes, I bumbled my way to success without a decent business plan. But why waste all the time, money and energy I did? Start your business plan *right now*, on that yellow pad you've got right beside you. Don't worry about the details; just begin investigating the sorts of things you'll be doing eventually.

Granted, some of us make plans and schedules that are more, well, "fluid" than others, but we all make plans for work, family and community events. We organize our own time and coordinate with others. Some of us even check to see if we're staying on schedule!

You've got at least one *crazy idea*. Maybe, like me, you want to "Make something and sell it!" Honestly, that was my whole business plan. For that, I risked our family's savings. The upside of my very minimal business plan? It didn't interfere with my creative, innovative side. The down side? I made up everything as I went along, one mistake at a time. It was like walking into a dark room and bumping into the furniture:

Ouch!	Quality Control in Manufacturing
Hey!	Importing from overseas
What the heck!	Warehousing and Distribution
Whoa!	Client Management

Without a plan or guide, I had to invent each step of a process that had already been honed and tested by others. I could have taken advantage of their experience, but that just wasn't my way. As an artist, I embraced randomness – even intentional randomness – to force me to find new connections, oddball solutions, unique outcomes. For instance, when playing the mountain dulcimer, I would sometimes purposefully un-tune the strings and play as if the instrument was in tune. The "wrong" notes forced me to experience familiar sounds in new ways. I also wanted to do everything myself, like I always had. Have I mentioned that I was stubborn?

What I didn't know, since I never asked anyone, was that a business plan could be constructed so that it would support my creative side and not interfere with my peculiar way of experiencing and interpreting the world.

Like my wife said, "Making a plan will force you to figure out where you want to end up and what you have to do to get there. You can check and see whether you're on the right track or not, and adjust things if you need to." She was right, but I was too excited and naïve to know it then. I thought I was ready, though nearly planless, to conquer the world.

Do I now wish I had had a more structured plan? Yup!
And that I had followed it? Oh yeah.

We could have avoided some magnificent blunders* and been twice as successful financially. *(See the chapter $297,372.61)*

When non-artists envision 'the artist's life,' their eyes glaze over with fantasies:

- Oh, you follow your inner muse
- You dance to the beat of your own drummer
- You know the secret handshake
- Your creativity flows all the time
- You can do whatever you want whenever you want

Well, sometimes.

Do you lean towards the creative side? Are you, like many creative types, addicted to excitement, discovery, and stimulation? Are you obsessive, rebellious and moody? Do you refuse rules? Are you easily bored? Do you suffer from ADIWTATAT (Attention Deficit "I Want That and That And That")? When you think of plans, do you scoff, "Fuggeddabowdit?"

If you tip more towards creative than linear, what solution might work for you? First, get advice from people who know their stuff.

"But I like to do everything myself."

That's great for doing "personal" creative work (think: little or no income). But for developing and producing products, making them in various locations, managing a worldwide distribution network and maintaining an office with employees, some solid advice is in order.

Nine years into my art-products venture, I did make a plan. This plan led to the successful sale of the bulk of that business, and I moved on to other things. But that was after my most magnificent blunder, among others.

The funny thing is, I ended up doing all of the things that would have been in a business plan, but by the seat of my pants, and only as each step became critical. I reinvented the wheel numerous times and wasted time and resources through duplication, overlap, confusion and mistakes.

We managed to stay in the game, but it was a miracle. Make – and follow – a plan! You can always change it; you're in charge, not the plan. Think of your business plan as a map. A map doesn't make you go anywhere, but it helps you make decisions about which way to turn, and it lets you check to make sure you're headed toward your destination

Take Action!

Ok, there are business plans, and then there are Business Plans. It can be as simple as, "I'm Gonna Make Something and Sell it!", or as thorough as the very detailed outline of the seven major components explained on Entrepreneur.com (see exact web site in Resources). A good deal of a formal business plan addresses financials, meaning your strategy for capitalization and growth coupled with a detailed overall analysis of cost versus return…makes sense. In running my business, I spent most of my time with the mechanics of design, manufacturing, client contact and product delivery. Because I was flush with cash from the early success of my *crazy idea*, I didn't see any need to do financial planning. I know…you're screaming out loud: "WHAT? How stupid is that?" Well, looking back, pretty stupid.

From my experience, apart from the really detailed financial stuff, the following are topics and questions that I would consider important when planning out how to carry your *crazy idea* into the real world. Please note that a lot of this is based on product introduction. But even with a service or an internal company innovation, you still need a plan and these suggestions can be beginning points for moving forward.

My further advice is to look at the article I referenced above at Entrepreneur.com, check out some other web suggestions for the *essential elements of a business plan*, speak to an actual, experienced person about business plan outlines, and then kick it into high gear:

- ◉ Make – and follow – a plan! You can always change it.
- ◉ State your *crazy idea*.

Then answer these questions:

- ☑ Labor: Who's going to do all the work?
- ☑ Potential customers: Who needs or wants your product?
- ☑ Direct competition: Who is already selling the same thing in the same market?
- ☑ Indirect competition: Who is building your market by selling similar, but non-competing products?
- ☑ Marketing: How is the world going to find out about your product?
- ☑ Price Point: If there's something like your product already on sale, what's the price? Will yours seem like a better deal for the price?
- ☑ Sources: Who will make your product?
- ☑ Capitalization: How will you get the money to produce and sell your product?
- ☑ Profit: when do you need to start making it?
- ☑ Distribution: How will your products get where they need to be?
- ☑ Sales: Who is going to get your goods into stores, catalogs, websites etc? Warehousing: Where are you going to keep your goods and who will track shipments?
- ☑ Admin? Who's going to keep track of all the financial, process and personnel details?
- ☑ Evaluation and next steps: How will you know how you're doing? How will you decide what to do next?
- ☑ Growth-what is your plan for success?
- ☑ The future-you want to do this forever?

12. Help!

 Fishtip™: Remember a time when you looked back at something you did and wished you had asked for help. Don't let this be another of those times...ask now.

There is unlimited help for entrepreneurs, some free, some fee. Businesses (sometimes even direct competitors) want – no, need – others to succeed. Our local, national and global economies are interlinked.

So ask for help. As you meet with other businesspeople, they will ask you questions that will help you understand not just the marketplace, but your own business. Be honest with your goals and needs, and listen with an open mind. Take lots of notes, make sure to thank them and keep them updated on your progress. And remember to help others when you are in a position to do so.

Organizations

B2B Networking Events are specifically designed to foster a climate of mutual help and growth. Every business needs products and services to maintain themselves and to grow...why not help each other? Look up **Yellow Tie International** on the web.

The Better Business Bureau is a non-governmental umbrella organization with local offices throughout the US and elsewhere. Accreditation by BBB means you are a trustworthy business. BBB member companies contractually agree to and adhere to the organization's high standards of ethical business behavior. BBB provides objective advice, free Business Reliability Reports and Charity Wise Giving Reports, plus educational information on topics affecting marketplace trust. To further promote trust, BBB also offers complaint and dispute resolution support for consumers and businesses. BBB charges membership fees.

CEO Roundtables offer ways to engage in stimulating and insight-filled discussions with business peers. Meetings are characterized by mutual trust, candor and confidentiality. You will find them in all areas of the country. Members of a local group may have related or dissimilar businesses. Either way, meetings offer a unique way to share concerns with others in similar situations. Advice offered is based on real life experience; the networking often creates more business opportunities – and the meetings can be fun. You may also form your own business roundtable to collectively solve problems. The big shots do it; you can too.

Colleges and Universities Entrepreneurship is 'hot' and now taught at over 2,000 colleges nationwide. Check first with your local community colleges for classroom and online classes and workshops.

Online business classes can provide just the advice you need. You can choose from a very wide variety of topics and work on your own schedule. No driving, no dress code. No face-to-face discussion either, though some online classes do include phone, video or real-time blog discussions.

Local Business Incubators Consider joining an incubator where some resources like office space and support are already set up. You'll need less money to get started, there are often advisors, and you get to mingle with other start-ups. Most cities have incubators.

Small Business Administration This federal government department offers programs and services to help you start, grow and succeed in business. An amazing array of resources, a great place to start. Just by browsing their website you'll see all kinds of things you'll want to learn. (See Resources)

<u>Individuals</u>

Mentors are working people or retirees who have been through it all and are happy to show you the ropes. They are like coaches, but often have direct experience in your field. They may set challenges and assign homework. They'll expect you to be serious about making progress and they'll hope that you'll mentor someone someday. Buy them lunch. See www.score.org in Resources.

Non-competing business leaders understand that usually, as the whole economy goes, so goes their business. Non-competing businesses have everything to gain and little to lose by helping

Selling The Scream

you, and they'll likely learn about their own business while advising you. Buy them lunch.

Trusted friends want you to succeed. Think about your friends' skills, experiences and personalities and target your questions accordingly. Be specific about what you need. Ask friends to contact you periodically and cheer you on. Buy them lunch.

Professional Life and Business Coaches help you identify and analyze your current situation and goals, and will help you make and follow a plan. They charge for their services. And, if they really help you reach your dream, buy them dinner.

Media

Print and online business articles can teach you a lot. Read the *NY Times*, the *Wall Street Journal*, and your local papers. You can subscribe to online editions and even have tailored information delivered via email. Try print and online. Clip and print articles of interest and keep them in a binder. Read through them once a week or once a month.

Self help books like this one cover every topic imaginable. Get recommendations from the people and organizations on this list. Read reviews. Then read – or listen – to several books. *Be discerning:* if everyone's advice worked, we'd all be at peace, in love, slender and rich.

Google "Entrepreneurship" and "Innovation" and the floodgates will open. Bookmark your favorite sites and visit often.

> *"Help, I need somebody / Help, not just anybody / Help, you know I need someone / Help!"*
>
> The Beatles
> *Musicians*

"One of things I keep learning is that the secret of being happy is doing things for other people."

Dick Gregory
Comedian, social activist, writer and entrepreneur

"I've learned that people will forget what you said, people will forget what you did, but people will never forget how you made them feel."

Maya Angelou
Memoirist and poet

"Dreams sometimes do come true. But not without something that looks a lot like hard work."

Sylvia Ashton Warner
New Zealand writer, poet and educator

Secret #3
All you have to do is ask.

Take Action!

- ▶ Ask around to get suggestions for a mentor. Trade organizations are a good place to start.

- ▶ Take a Business Basics class from a community college or university. This will give you some ground to stand on.

- ▶ Join or form a group of peers in business. You will be invaluable aids to each other when problems arise.

> "People ask what gives me the authority to give advice? I say, First of all, I don't give advice. Dr. Phil gives advice. Mr. T. helps people. I motivate them, I inspire them, I give them hope, and I plant the seed so they can feel good about themselves."
>
> Mr. T.
> *Really Genuine and Cool Guy,*
> *Media Personality*

Selling The Scream

Finding your Niche: Marketing and Sales

Before you start calling factories in China or working with Fair Trade organizations in Central America, make sure there's a market for your ideas.

13. How will you get your *CRAZY IDEA* out there?

 Fishtip™: Identify your most likely customers. *Target them first, but don't stop there!*

 Fishtip™: Send information and samples to specific people. *Get current contact information.*

 Fishtip™: Be creative when searching for niche sales opportunities. *Look sideways.*

 Fishtip™: Create a mythology around your product. Get the public to help. *Make it a phenomenon.*

Yes, you've already looked over the topics included in an entire business plan. You may have jotted down some preliminary ideas about how to accomplish all those steps. Take a serious look at sales and marketing. Marketing is getting your idea out there. Sales is the actual mechanics of getting it sold. Your idea has no value if people don't know about it.

Why do people buy stuff?

As you shape your *crazy idea* to appeal to the marketplace, it helps to know why people buy things. The more of those reasons your product or service provides, the greater the likelihood of a sale.

People buy a product that:
- meets a real, practical need
- saves money
- makes life easier
- is Green, helps the environment
- makes an emotional connection: it makes people feel a way they like to feel (safe, attractive, loved, nostalgic, superior, surprised, included, righteous, understood, smart, entertained, prosperous, amused, cool, hip....)
- benefits a third party, charity or cause

⦿ may win them something

The more benefits your product provides, the easier it will be to sell. And people like choices. When they can choose between red, blue, green and black socks, they're more likely to place a bigger combined order.

Stake out your **niche**. Make sure your product is unique in the marketplace, and offer choices if you can, so customers are choosing from amongst your product variations, rather than choosing between your product and your competitor's similar product.

Why did people buy our stuff?

There weren't many inflatables out there in 1991 besides pool toys or knock-over clowns for toddlers, and there certainly weren't any other fine art inflatables, the *Scream* or otherwise. Our inflatable *Scream* was in no way a necessity like food or medical care, but it did surprise, amuse and entertain people. And because we offered lots of choices, so rather than thinking, "Do I want a *Scream*?", potential customers were more likely to think, "Do I want a big *Scream*, a medium *Scream* or a small *Scream*?" Then they would pick the one that was just right.

People bought inflatable *Screams* partly because it became a phenomenon. It became cool to have one; *Scream* owners were the art-smart, fun, in-crowd!

January 27, 1992
By Hans Hjellemo

Reprinted with permission of Hans Hjellemo and Dagens Næringsliv

Edvard Munch's "The Scream" is literally roaring ahead in the US. The human-sized inflatable version has caught on particularly well as a décor accent for psychiatrists and American businessmen. The actress Jodie Foster also received one as a birthday gift.

Selling The Scream

While the Munch Museum here at home has taken years to decide whether to allow Munch's lithographs to be printed on T-shirts, On The Wall Productions Inc in the US has sold over 2,000 inflatable versions of "The Scream" just since they launched the product on October 31.

"The inflatable 'Scream' has been a big hit. It's selling well in the US, and has also done well in Australia," says Robert Fishbone, the director of the company On The Wall Productions.

"Originally we reproduced and painted a 180 cm high "Scream" on a wall. The idea of producing "The Scream" as a balloon in an inflatable human version came from a friend."

The in thing for psychiatrists

"People buy 'The Scream' to give to children, and a lot of psychiatrists want to have it in their offices because 'The Scream' expresses the darkest powers that ravage people's emotional lives. Other people want to have it as a surprising and original item in the office, while others keep it at home or take it to the beach," Robert Fishbone said.

The American "Scream" has been sold through friends and friends of friends, but now Robert Fishbone is setting out to find businesses that want to sell the inflatable version of Edvard Munch's immortal and perhaps most famous subject.

He claims to have the law on his side, but the Munch Museum argues that the reproduction is illegal. Regardless, Robert Fishbone gets letters every day about what different customers use Munch's celebrity for.

"We believe 'The Scream' will maintain its place in the market for several years, and that our version is something more than a fad.

"The shape is good and the painting is nice," Robert Fishbone says.

(Note: not all of the facts are entirely accurate, but the general gist is.)

Permit me to time-travel and digress for the sake of a good story:

after we were deep into manufacturing the inflatable *Scream*, that crazy product got a lot of world publicity (more on all that later), and we started getting fan mail. People sent unsolicited pictures and stories describing why they liked the *Scream* inflatable, or who gave it to them, or whom they gave it to, or how they used it or where they saw one.... The submissions were so, well, weird and cool and compelling that we set up an online museum called the **Screameria**. We posted people's photographs and anecdotes, and added additional features to the site:

- Send an e-postcard with an audio scream
- Listen to famous movie screams
- Vote on the gender of the screamer in Munch's painting
- Listen to a reading of the passage from Munch's diary where he described his inspiration for the painting

The site's up again at www.robertfishbone.com. Check it out and email any new text, images or Scream tidbits to scream@robert fishbone.com. Some of our favorite submissions are in this book.

We identified our target market: people likely to know about Munch's *"The Scream,"* and we marketed accordingly. But wait. Buying *Screams* wasn't just about being art-smart. After selling around forty thousand *Scream* inflatables it became clear that not everyone who bought the product knew that it was based on a famous artwork. In fact only half of the people who bought it knew about Munch's painting, *"The Scream."* The other half of the population? When they saw it they had a powerful, emotional response, something like, "Yeah, that's EXACTLY how I feel."

Our sales numbers taught us that most of us get frustrated, and most of us could use a good laugh. We came up with a tag line, "If you can't make life any better, make it funnier with the *Scream* inflatable. It'll understand you when no one else will." Those sales numbers also taught us that our market was much bigger than we thought. With this in mind, I pitched our product to Lifestyle editors at newspapers and received publicity that went well beyond the museum crowd. I also looked for stores that catered to hip, edgy shoppers and got into such chains as Urban Outfitters, Claire's Boutique, and Spencer's Gifts.

From The Screameria:

Dear *Scream* Museum:

I acquired my *Scream, Jr.* in mid-December, 1995, at the time of my Christmas tree decorating. Since I had been furloughed twice in the last two months as a 'nonessential' federal employee, I felt my *Scream*-buddy was an appropriate topping for my tree. As you can see in the picture, it really sets the mood for the season. *Scream*-buddy now adorns my cubicle at work. Yes, we did finally return to our challenging, though nonessential job.

Thanks and Best Wishes, Anne T.

❡   ❡   ❡

From an employee at a Wisconsin company

Enclosed please find a few photos of our *Scream, Jr.* He adorns our office Christmas tree, reflecting the mood of many at this time of year. We have entitled him "*Scream* Angel". Our office, located in the northernmost part of Wisconsin, has a large percentage of employees of Norwegian descent. They, unfortunately, do not realize that this is a satiric commentary on the ironic and frantic commercialism of this season of 'peace'. Rather, they actually seem to like this year's tree.

Go figure, Jon C.

❡   ❡   ❡

An email from Eva D.

I heard that some time back, scientists were thinking about burying some hellacious nuclear waste in the New Mexico desert. They were going to cement over it, etc, etc, but wanted to be sure that no one would ever try to open up the waste dumps, for obvious reasons…but they wanted to use a universal 'sign' rather than a warning in English or other language. They thought of the famous red circle with the line through it, some other things which denote "NO!", but they decided to use a concrete cast impression of 'The Scream'…they decided that it was pretty universal, even for people who couldn't read or write. Smart, no?

❂   ❂   ❂

Memo from the Sausalito Ferry Gift Shop

Customer was asked to leave the store because he wouldn't stop hitting his friends with a *Scream*, Jr.

14. How can you get people to buy your stuff?

You must claim – and then communicate – your product niche. Few items appeal to everybody. With this in mind, it is best to target a niche for your product or service. Here's an example:

Jess Bachman created a poster a few years ago called **Death and Taxes™**, a striking visual representation of how tax dollars are allocated and spent. Basically, the size of the circle on the poster relates to the amount of money allocated by the federal government to the department or program. He reissues it every year with updated fiscal information.

Jess wanted to sell more posters but just couldn't determine the best way to get them into stores. I suggested that in addition to focusing on the general gift market, he could target other industries that might be interested in the poster, such as tax accountants, college stores, political organizations, government agencies, as well as specialty catalogs.

He was already working with a **fulfillment house** so he did not have to handle the goods himself. This was a real cost and time saver and allowed him to focus on finding new sales opportunities, a much better use of his time.

He knew that he would make more money in the long run by writing larger orders, even if it meant less profit per piece. Right away he picked up an order from a catalog/website catering to geeks, exactly the type of reseller he wanted. Since it is a poster, more people in that niche as well as their wider circle of friends and associates will be seeing it thus spreading the word, leading to more sales, and hopefully reorders from the catalog.

When he released a new poster in early 2009, he capitalized on **social media** and other forms of web marketing and sold 400 units in two weeks…those are great numbers.

To take it even further, he made a visualization of the February, 2009 U.S. stimulus package for *The Atlantic* magazine. He states and I totally agree, "It always helps to sell a product AND a service, the cross promotional and marketing is fantastic."

Besides marketing our *Screams* to museums, I looked for organizations that catered to people who might be stressed. Well, heck, that's everyone. Lucky me! *The Scream* works for people going through transitions: relationship, school, work. Again, that covers a lot of territory. My focus became the media that served these groups. This usually meant magazines (remember, this was before the web took off). I sent free samples to editors, writers and photographers along with a witty letter talking about the *Scream's* relevance to the readers in "these stressful times."

Free samples are one of your best marketing tools. My friend Scott Ginsberg, who speaks on "Approachability," said that if you don't give away 500 of your first printing of 1,000 books you are not doing a proper marketing job. He's right. Relative to the cost of your product (assuming you're not going to sell airplanes or diamond rings), the potential returns are enormous. There's nothing like someone holding the real deal in their hands to convey how cool your *crazy idea* really is. Make sure though that you identify a particular person of influence to send it to, not just, for instance, "End of Year Gift Writer" and make sure your information is current. Packages without a current name are usually delivered to the mailroom where someone has to make a decision on who gets it. Don't make the mailroom guess, or your sample will end up in the circular file, on the desk of someone who can't help you, or in the mail clerk's pocket.

Take Action!

▶ Who can you send a sample to who can help your business? TV talk show hosts all promote products they think are cool, weird or actually practical. Send them yours.

▶ If you are selling a product, go visit potential outlets, either stores or online; anything like yours already there? How is yours better?

▶ What service can you make out of your *crazy idea* product? This is called being an expert.

▶ What products can you make to complement your service? This is called merchandising.

- ▶ If you offer a service, offer yourself as an expert on radio, TV, in print media, online. Become the go-to person.
- ▶ Remember that the media loves a story: make yours compelling.

> *"Anything we do in advertising is controversial. If it's provocative and sensual and related to what we're selling, I'm willing to take the chance. I have fun with the ads."*
>
> Calvin Klein
> *Fashion Designer*

> *"Many a small thing has been made large by the right kind of advertising."*
>
> Mark Twain
> *Author and Humorist*

Selling The Scream

Secret #4
Don't blend in.

Make your product different on the shelf, in catalogs, online and in customers' minds.

 Fishtip™: Don't be surprised: Once you start putting your product out there, you are no longer in total control. Your product can take on a life of its own.

You've created/found your unique niche. Your amazing new Salsa really is better than the other kinds available. But how are customers going to know that?

On the shelf and in catalogs, what differentiates your Salsa from the other 999 bottles of red sauce? *Online*, with everything looking similar on a computer screen, how can you make what you offer jump out? How can you make your site rise to the top of a search? In other words, how are you going to get your *crazy idea* to stand out *in customers' minds* and how are you making it easy for customers to find you and buy your product or service.

Today, the Internet gives you incredible abilities to search for niche groups for your *crazy idea*. First, see what else out there might be similar to your idea and target the same customers. Promote why yours is not just different, but better. Refer back to page 49-50 and see how many benefits your product provides. Brainstorm who might fit in your target niche: clubs, special interest groups, hobbyists, collectors, agencies, business associations, social networking connections. Then start Googling those words along with your product idea and I guarantee you'll end up with so many possible buyers that you'll wonder where you are going to get the time to contact them all. And read *"The Future"* in this book.

To make an initial contact, I would often send inflated *Scream*, Jrs. to prospective buyers who would take it out of the box and put it on their desk. The reaction was instantaneous, and when others walked by and exclaimed "I need that, right now," the sale was made, the article was written. Drama has its place.

While I didn't really know that much about how to efficiently run a business, I did know how to attract attention and tell people about things. I knew how to say the same thing in a variety of ways so that various people would get a similar meaning from the message.

It's like the **Theory of Multiple Intelligences**, developed by Howard Gardener. Research has shown that people learn in different ways. Some people are analytical, some learn better through music, or movement, or kinesthetically or interpersonally. The trick is being able to use all those pathways simultaneously so that everyone in a group is being spoken to.

As a public artist, musician and performer I had beaucoup experience in communicating with people, and often had to improvise. I especially enjoyed catching people by surprise, opening new doors, twisting rigid concepts and bending reality.

What was my plan, then, for marketing the *Scream*? Frankly, I was so excited when I received my first shipment of products that I just wanted folks to have them. I rushed down to the public library, found a reference book and wrote down addresses for some magazines and college art departments. Then I went home (World Headquarters was the extra room downstairs), and packed individual *Screams*. I gave them to the postal carrier, then stood at the door and waved goodbye as they made their way out into the world. "GOOD LUCK!" Call it scatter-shot marketing....

What was I thinking? I didn't even have specific contact names to send those samples to. The funny thing though.... Things worked out. Our *Scream* inflatables blew people's minds!

Selling The Scream

Take Action!

▶ Brainstorm the unique attributes of your product, especially any emotional connections.

▶ Brainstorm ways to add/strengthen benefits. What's unique about your product? How is it different from other products already for sale? How can you increase that uniqueness and/or make it more obvious and desirable?

▶ How can you get the public excited enough about your product so that they'll help you market it?

▶ How can you give customers choices?

▶ Identify who will clearly benefit the most from your product. Target them first. Then research how to access them. Follow up right away.

▶ Who else will be interested in your product and how can you reach them? (Get out the sunscreen. You're going to spend some serious time surfing –the web!)

▶ Send samples to selected media and to a few other choice recipients who look like a match. Are there any events, holidays, life transitions, or news stories you can tie into? (I found a holiday called *"International Moment of Frustration Scream Day."*)

15. How will you sell your stuff?

 Fishtip™: If you work with sales reps, draft detailed, written contracts with specified time periods.

 Fishtip™: If it doesn't work out with a particular rep group, try another. It's just like any other relationship.

I arranged with my cousin Jeffrey Horner, who worked in ribbon sales, to get some **sales reps**. In my field, the gift industry, they earn a 15% commission on the order total. They showed our *Scream* around and wrote orders for about 20 stores. Each order had to be for a minimum of six pieces and they had to pay **COD**. Two months later our goods arrived. I very excitedly packed the first orders, drove over to UPS and dropped them off.

Sales reps* are a convenient way to have your products shown around, but the devil is in the details. Reps must be held accountable with sales goals and timelines. Remember, you are hiring them to work for you. Of course, since their income is all based on sales commissions they have an incentive to do a great job. But, if they don't produce, if they don't follow up with clients, if they don't go after the re-order, let them go and find a better match. But make sure to have a written contract with them, stipulating grounds for ending the relationship. It's like having a get-out-of-business-free card.

Reps prefer to have a line of products to show to store owners, not just a single item like our Scream inflatable. But because our product was so totally unique, both the Reps and stores decided to give it a shot.

One week after those first 20 orders were placed, a San Francisco store called. The owner remarked: "When I spoke with your rep I said your things were pretty weird, but there's nothing else like 'em, so maybe they would sell, maybe not, and I took six? Well, I'll take 60 more; they're hot!"

The same thing started happening everywhere: not only were our original stores re-ordering frequently, but other store owners, who had seen them, wanted them for their shops. Media coverage soon followed. It was our first experience with what would become known as **viral marketing**. Today, viral marketing refers to "marketing techniques that use pre-existing social networks to produce increases in brand awareness or to achieve other marketing objectives, like product sales, through processes similar to the spread of pathological and computer viruses." In our case it started as word-of-mouth and took on a life of its own.

I can distinctly recall our checking account balance growing over those first three months of sales. In our first full year, we sold over three hundred thousand dollars of just one product –a 54-inch tall inflatable *Scream* – who would have thought!

"I can *definitely* do this!"

Traditional Sales and Marketing

People have been trading and selling things since, well, a really long time ago. Selling face to face wherever you happened to be. Banging on drums and bells, blowing trumpets and shouting were the first attention getting devices, used to call people to events, fairs and the marketplace. The printed word followed. Pre-web print methods of advertising/selling ranged from newspapers, mailers, magazines, coupons and flyers to billboards, posters and printed garments and balloons. Eventually, advertising expanded to include radio, TV, trade shows and special events…even sky writers.

Back in ancient (pre-Internet) times when we started selling *Screams*, the sales reps actually visited potential clients. They also exhibited at trade shows. Between my scattershot approach of blindly sending *Screams* to unknown parties and the sales that came in through the reps, our bank account grew.

Viral Sales and Marketing

As we developed new products, we continued to get media coverage. It helped that our first product caused deep emotional responses. Remember that people are more likely to buy something if they have an emotional attachment to it.

While I did do a LOT of "traditional" PR and publicity marketing for the *Scream* inflatable, I look back now and see that things really took off when the *Scream* went viral, even though, again, it started out pre-web.

But it was when the print media picked up on it, that some **luck** came my way. Every editor and writer and critic remembered the painting *The Scream* from their Art 101 class in college…and they thought our product was too cool to pass up. This resulted in newspaper articles and pictures across the country featuring our *Scream* inflatable. Our biggest break came when the *New York Times* ran a picture and story, and since most other papers and periodicals also read the *New York Times*, word spread fast, and requests for information followed. Articles are free advertising.

We (the *Scream* inflatable and I) were in *People* magazine (yup, I really did make it into *People*). We were in the *Wall Street Journal* and *The Washington Post*, plus lots of magazines: *Vogue, Smithsonian, Time, New Yorker, Entrepreneur, Success, Financial World*, and even *Playboy* (no, not the centerfold).

Playboy had a brief mention of our product on their back page, calling it the "Beautiful Screamer"…pretty clever. A few days later, the phone calls started, first during the day, then in the middle of the night. Those who actually spoke asked things like; "So, what kind of inflatable is…it?" Some callers just breathed heavy. While robbed of sleep, my wife and I enjoyed being entertained, and we did sell quite a few *Screams* from that titillating mention.

Movies and TV shows began asking to use our *Screams* for set dressing: *The Cosby Show, CBS News, Paramount Pictures*. President Clinton's Press Secretary used a *Scream*, Jr. to begin a briefing…. Comedian Richard Lewis appeared with them in *People*. Michael Feldman gives them away on his *Wha D'Ya Know* radio show. People were screaming to buy *Screams*!

It's been smooth sailing ever since, and my wife and I are rich and lazy. Not! There were bumps in the road ahead. But before we bash along those bumps, and assuming you've made great progress on your sales and marketing plan, let's go back to the rest of your business plan, the nitty-gritties of managing production, office admin and all that fun stuff.

How will you sell your stuff?   65

Take Action!

▶ Attend a trade show and speak to prospective rep groups. Just let them know why you want to speak to them right away.

▶ If you don't already have one, build a great website that is memorable and easy to understand. Make it content-rich, and keep it fresh with new material. Have friends try it out.

▶ Send free samples to the media and famous people. You never know when someone will fall in love with your *crazy idea* and want to make you rich and famous.

▶ Remember that the media likes a story, so be prepared with a good one.

👁 👁 👁

Free publicity is fantastic, but at some point you should look at paid advertising including Google Ad Words and other similar services. The main reasons to advertise are to let people know about you or your offering, and to keep letting them know: Out of sight, out of mind. But at some point you have to determine if the advertising is paying off, meaning, generating sales. You'll want to establish some way of analyzing the return on that investment. Understand what kind of return you need to break even, and to become profitable. Like all the other components of your business, you'll want to have this be a part of your official plan, probably under marketing. There are individuals and companies that specialize in marketing plans. It may be worth it to at least seek out a free consultation.

16. Look what time it is!

 Fishtip™: If a client agrees to place a large order, get a PO in writing.

 Fishtip™: Plan ahead. Way, way ahead.

In sales and marketing, and therefore in manufacturing and shipping, timing is everything. Let's look at sales and marketing now. The bulk of gift items and household goods are sold in the fourth quarter of the calendar year, also known as Q4, also known as the Holiday Season. If you are selling any type of gift item, consider showing it at the big gift shows.

The biggest US gift shows are the New York Gift Show, usually held in January and August, and the American International Toy Fair, held in NYC each February. You may be a perfect fit for the gigantic Consumer Electronics Show in Las Vegas. There are a myriad of other shows serving every conceivable industry, and they're held throughout the year in a variety of locations besides NYC and Las Vegas: Los Angeles, Chicago, Orlando, San Francisco, Houston, Atlanta, Gatlinburg, TN... and more. I exhibited at the Museum Store show. There are also international shows. Museum Expressions and Maison et Objets in Paris and Musicmesse in Frankfurt were important for us. Search **trade shows** online.

For my industry, gifts, we exhibit in January and August. January is a good time to show new merchandise, August is when people write their final orders for the holiday season. This means that you have to time things so that you have adequate inventory to not just meet current orders, but any re-orders that may come in. It is very tricky since you never know how well your product will sell. This is of course only a problem with hard goods ordered in bulk. Software and web based services are different topics entirely, as is **on-demand goods** *(see The Future is Now).*

You need to know how long it will take to manufacture your goods, how long it will take for them to arrive to your location and how long it will take to process your clients' orders. You need to know what factors may delay any stage of this process. Holidays cause guaranteed delays; in particular, **Chinese New Year.** Typically, factories close for two weeks at Chinese New Year, so nothing gets done. Nothing. No matter what.

Weather can close factories, but you can't know about that, nor can you know what political or environmental issues might affect your business. The upshot is that you want to build as much extra time as possible into the process to ensure you can fill your orders.

Plan Ahead. Way, way ahead. Most clients have a **cancel date** on their orders; they won't wait forever, so it's often better to spend a little more on storage for unsold goods than to not have product to fill orders (unless you'll be left with lots of un-sellable seasonal, holiday or client-specific goods).

Know what holidays can interfere with manufacturing in another country. Sign up for and read shippers' newsletters to see about any upcoming delays from possible union negotiations, train problems or weather or fuel situations. Get an estimate from your shipper listing ALL costs. The shipping quote will be good for usually 30 days; then they may revise it.

If a client agrees to buy a large portion of a factory order, get a firm PO in writing. It won't protect you if the client goes out of business, but it will otherwise obligate them to accept and pay for the goods. Another safeguard is **sellers insurance**, which I never had occasion to buy, but check it out if large sums of money are at stake…ask someone in your trade if they think it is worthwhile.

There are many factors that can contribute to your success or failure with the movement of your goods from factory to buyer. Like everything else, the more you know, the better prepared you will be to maximize your profits and minimize your losses. And have I mentioned "Plan ahead?"

Take Action!

▶ Call or visit a shipping company and have an informational meeting. If you are a possible new account they will be more than happy to share everything they know with you. Ask them what you are forgetting. In fact, ask this question of everyone you ask for advice.

▶ If you haven't already, attend a trade show, the bigger the better. You will see more and learn more than you thought possible.

▶ Talk to a few folks who have manufactured goods and get them to tell you their horror stories and what you could do to minimize your risks.

> *"You can't overestimate the need to plan and prepare. In most of the mistakes I've made, there has been this common theme of inadequate planning beforehand. You really can't over-prepare in business!"*
>
> Chris Corrigan
> *Australian businessman*

Selling The Scream

Making It Happen: Business Mechanics

The nitty-gritties of managing production, office administration and all that fun stuff

Selling The Scream

17. Are you going to make stuff in your basement, or what?

 Fishtip™: You can't do everything yourself.

 Fishtip™: Work with people and companies you trust. Get recommendations from someone you already know and trust.

 Fishtip™: Do unto others as you would have them do unto you.

You never know when - or which - offhand comment will change the direction of your life. I had no idea how to get inflatable *Screams* made. Rummaging in the file cabinets of my left brain, I stumbled upon Cabinet 216. In drawer 3, halfway towards the back in a battered folder, were notes from a conversation ten years earlier: Acme Premium Supply had offered to help us produce our *crazy ideas*.

Acme assured us, "Yeah, we can make an inflatable. Send us some drawings so we can see what you have in mind." A month later they called to say that our sample inflatable *Scream* was done. Our museum products business had officially begun!

Acme saved me from having to find and negotiate with an over-seas manufacturer myself. How would I have known where to look, who to trust, how to monitor quality, set terms, handle packaging, manage importing…. Acme handled all that. They took a financial cut, of course, but in return we essentially had a bank-rolled busi-ness partner.

Eventually, I started doing everything myself, from working with the manufacturer to importing and distribution, and our profit margin went up by 40%, but at the beginning, sharing profits with Acme was a terrific deal for both of us.

Work with someone you trust. Even if you haul yourself to the fac-tory (probably in another country) and meet all the other parties concerned, you'll need a 'partner' that can take care of things at that end. This can be a **trading partner**. They usually do not own any factories themselves but will help connect you with the appropriate facility as well as aid in the shipment of your goods. Make sure they oversee quality control during production and that the samples you approve are the same as what is shipped. Hold them accountable (get it in writing). They usually get a better deal from the factory, so your cost will likely be the same as if you had dealt with the factory yourself.

Assemble a team of potential advisors. Maintain good files to keep track of people and organizations you already know and trust, and what they can offer. To meet more manufacturers and suppliers, go to trade shows. These events take place all over the world, all the time. Or visit **show rooms**, which are found in every major world city.

Things have changed since way back when Acme made that first *Scream*. Then, businesses communicated by fax, phone and even snail mail! It was more personal and much slower. Today, most people do business online and on the phone, but in the end, it is still the quality of your personal relationships that get things done. Or not.

Today, you may be able to take advantage of an easy-entry manufacturing approach that didn't even exist when I started: on-demand production. If, for instance, you want to sell custom-printed t-shirts, websites like cafepress.com are a low risk and easy way to start up a small business. Ponoko.com in New Zealand can make plastic and wooden furniture for you. In fact, except for doing your design, these new ventures can handle many aspects of your business operation. *(See Business in the Internet Age and Resources for more information regarding on-demand production.)*

Heads Up: There are all kinds of regulations, old and very new, regarding manufacturing, especially concerning international imports. Problems with product safety, chemical contamination, insect infestation and using endangered woods have all made the process of bringing goods across borders more complicated. Governments will work with you to keep commerce flowing, but it will take perseverance and patience.

Take Action!

- ▶ Find people who have things manufactured domestically or overseas. Ask them for advice. Speak in generalities at first for each other's protection.

- ▶ Assemble a team of potential advisors.

- ▶ Constantly check for new laws and regulations governing manufacturing and materials composition. Ask shippers for their newsletters.

- ▶ Investigate on-demand manufacturers as a way to start. It's a low risk (low profit) way for you to get started, until you're ready for the higher risk, potentially higher profit, do-it-yourself approach.

Hey Wait! What if you are going to make stuff in your basement, or garage or kitchen or extra bedroom? What do you need to know?

Answer: the same information that any entrepreneur would need. Sure, you won't be importing from overseas but you'll still need a plan, a source for funds, a reliable source for your raw materials and supplies (even if it is your own garden or livestock), a legal structure for taxes and employees, some great advice from a mentor and a marketing plan which includes a dynamite and simple to understand website. Make it easy for people to find and buy your stuff. For further information about 'kitchen businesses' get a copy of *Mommy Millionaire: How I Turned My Kitchen Table Idea into a Million Dollars and How You Can, Too* by Kay Levine

Selling The Scream

18. Can you pick up the tab?

 Fishtip™: Get a banker. Patronize a local bank.

 Fishtip™: If the first bank turns you down, try, try again somewhere else.

 Fishtip™: Make sure to also check into credit unions.

That first *Scream* sample was great, so the next step was to get thousands made, right? No, the next step was coming up with the bucks to pay for that production run. Our family's life savings consisted of a $20,000 CD (as in Certificate of Deposit, not compact disc). "We can just use that," I assured my wife. Though visibly shaking at the idea, she agreed. What a woman!

The factory's **Minimum Ordering Quantity, or MOQ**, was 12,000 pieces, priced at much more than our CD. But ACME proposed that if we gave them the $20K as a down payment, they would go ahead with the order. They would handle all of the manufacturing and importing and would even help with warehousing, which was a good thing, since I knew absolutely nothing about any of that. Acme would give us $20K's worth of *Screams*, enough for us to get going, and then would sell us more as we could pay for them. It was a great deal. Acme took some of the risk; they were confident that we could actually pull this off.

If you don't have extra bucks stashed somewhere for start-up costs, try approaching family and friends as lenders or investors, or apply for a bank loan. If all else fails – and only then – you could run up your credit cards, but think long and hard before you do.

For bank loans, you'll need to make a strong case and you'll need collateral (how about your house?). If you apply for a bank loan, or even if you just need a place to stash your cash from other sources, develop a relationship with a personal banker. Your personal banker can be not just your loan officer but also an advisor. It's almost like having another member on your team, for free. They want you to be successful: not only will you repay the loan, but you may borrow more as you expand your business. Banks love this!

Two years into *Scream* production, I approached my local bank for a business loan. We'd painted murals for this bank so they knew us. I put together …OK, I'll admit it, my first business plan, showing our corporate structure, past sales, expected sales, new product introduction, press clippings, and personal assets. However, when I explained that we were selling inflatable *Screams*, I got that "speaking Klingon through a kazoo" look again. "You're selling *what*?"

Needless to say, that bank turned us down. I approached another local bank. The president collected art, the staff was young, and the institution was looking for new businesses to invest in. When I explained *Screams* to them, they said, "That is so cool. how much do you need?" and they gave me the requested amount, $90,000.

That first bank? They got bought up by a bigger bank that was bought by a bigger bank that was bought by a bigger bank that eventually absorbed my 'new' bank. Our loan was small potatoes for them and we dropped off their radar screen….until I started having major problems paying back our loan…but that's another story *(see $297,372.61)*.

Take Action!

▶ Calculate how much money you need.

▶ Plan and practice your pitch. Be prepared. Talk it through, but have written copies, too. Keep your initial pitch very simple; get it down to 2-3 sentences. This is sometimes called an 'elevator pitch', short enough so that you could explain your *crazy Idea* to someone while riding in an office building elevator. The goal is to get them to want to know more. There will be plenty of time to explain the details later once you get them hooked.

▶ Go to an **Idea Bounce** or Business Plan Competition at a local college. You'll learn a lot by watching how well, or not, others are prepared to clearly present their crazy ideas to a panel of judges. I've been a judge and it is an eye opening and sobering exercise.

▶ Patronize a local bank and get a personal banker. There

is a bank or an investor out there who will take an interest in your *crazy idea* and will help you grow your business. It may not be the first or second person you approach, but each meeting will give you a greater understanding of how to compellingly present yourself and pitch your *crazy idea*. Local banks have more interest in seeing neighborhood businesses grow.

▶ Look into working with **Credit Unions**. They often weather financial downturns better than banks and can be in a better position to offer small business loans.

Selling The Scream

19. How will you get your stuff from the factory?

 Fishtip™: Work with your manufacturer and shipper to determine timing. It is essential to keep timetables in mind.

 Fishtip™: Don't underestimate how long everything takes.

There are many ways to get goods from the factory to you, or to have them **drop shipped** from the factory directly to a client. If the factory is in the same country as the destination, you will likely ship by truck, either the whole truckload or **LTL**, less than a truck load.

Most likely these days, you goods will come from Asia, either by **ocean freight** or **air freight**. Air is quick but costs more. Consider air shipping a small portion of your order to check on quality, use as sales and marketing samples, and fill important, pressing orders right away.

With ocean freight, your goods go into a shipping container at a port, often as an **LCL**, less than a container load. The container is loaded on to a ship, crosses the ocean, is off-loaded onto a truck or train, and makes its way to you, perhaps going through other handling facilities. By this time your goods are likely on **pallets**.

Timing is so important, I'll say again: Don't underestimate how long everything takes. It is essential to keep timetables in mind. Work with your manufacturer and shipper to determine timing. It is easy and deadly to underestimate the time from sample approval to delivery into your hot, little hands.

Manufacturing, once a final sample is approved, can take 60 days or longer depending on the size of the order, the complexity of the goods and the time of year. You also may need to add 45-90 days additional if molds are part of the process. Reordering takes less time.

Ocean freight is economical but slow. For example, once full containers are loaded onto ships in Asia, it takes 30-45 days for goods to reach St. Louis. That doesn't include getting the stuff to and into the containers, or getting the stuff from the truck or train once it's in town.

Shipping goods between countries involves lots of paperwork: **Shippers Letter of Instructions, Commercial Invoice, Bill of Lading, Customs Brokerage forms, Packing Slip, Security forms**. Your shipper can help you with all of this. They're your partner in this part of the process.

Your shipper can also give you an accurate quote of what it will cost to ship/import goods. There are many fees, and they add up. Divide this total cost by the quantity of goods you are getting to determine what it adds to your cost of goods.

When you order a lot of something, you spread the shipping and importing costs over the whole order, lowering costs on each item. Of course, you'd better be confident you can sell all that stuff!

Take Action!

▶ Comparison shop shipping methods and shippers. You're comparing schedules and costs. As in other parts of your business, seek referrals from trusted sources.

▶ Make a timetable. Start with all the deadlines you already know for sure. Work with your manufacturer and shipper to determine timing. Include deadlines and consequences in your manufacturing and shipping contracts.

▶ Calculate how many items you'll need to ship right away, via air freight, for quality control, sales and marketing samples and important, pressing orders.

20. Where can you keep all of that stuff?

 Fishtip™: Consider using a distributor or fulfillment center to process and warehouse your products. If you do, check your inventory periodically.

 Fishtip™: Save samples from every manufacturing run in case discrepancies arise.

☑ You've roughed out your business plan.
☑ You've really delved into marketing and sales.
☑ Now let's dive into the rest of the details.

Your products are about to be delivered, but wait…where are you going to keep everything? Oops!

Let's assume that you are going to be processing orders yourself, or with your staff. You'll have some base of operations in your home or elsewhere. If your inventory takes up a lot of space, you will need some kind of warehouse, preferably in the same location as your office, keeping your operations as efficient as possible.

Home storage
Maybe you don't have a lot of inventory, or it just doesn't take up a lot of room. You probably could operate from your home, or a small office. You can then either have a shipping service pick up from your location, or just drop it off at the neighborhood UPS or Fedex store or the Post Office.

Storage in a separate space
If you have a lot of inventory, or it is big and just takes up a lot of room, you will likely either need a warehouse as part of your operations center, or you can rent space in someone else's warehouse, or more simply, in a **You Store It** type facility. Self storage is relatively inexpensive; there is likely one within a few miles of your office/home. I currently operate from my home and use a public storage facility for my excess Inventory.

Drop shipments
Depending on the merchandise and the client's order size, you

may be able to have orders drop shipped from the manufacturer or from a **fulfillment house**.

Manufacturers require a minimum order to make it worthwhile for them to prepare goods for drop shipping to another destination. They may also add on extra fees for preparation and delivery. You might be able to pass these costs on to your client. For instance, we typically split up our factory order of *Screams* and deliver a portion directly to my distributor in Japan.

Fulfillment House

A fulfillment house can warehouse your inventory, and take and process orders. Their fee is often based on the number of orders they will have to deal with, and how much work will be involved in picking, packing and shipping each order. **Accounts Payable and Receivable** are usually left to you.

Domestic Distributor

Or, you may find a domestic distributor. They can place an order through you for a large quantity of goods which they can take possession of overseas. They are then responsible for importing, warehousing and client management. You will not make as much money from the sales but you don't have to touch the goods at all. Finding the right distributor –someone you trust who will do an excellent job selling – is the key factor. Again, get recommendations from trusted friends or business associates. **Trophy Music Company** based in Cleveland, Ohio distributes my line of music products. It is a great deal for both the distributor and me.

Make sure your inventory is stored in a safe, secure, dry place. Does it have to be temperature controlled? Will you need a sprinkler system? Might it attract pests? What kind of access will you need? (You Store It facilities are usually closed during the night). Who pays utilities? You'll probably want insurance to cover the cost of your goods, and you'll need to do a hand count of your inventory as you receive it as well as monthly to make sure it agrees with whatever your computer system says you have. Sell the oldest merchandise first. Keep production runs separate in case there is a problem, such as a defect. This will allow you to track the specific products, not your entire warehouse. In fact, for this reason, current laws require special labeling which can include date and place of manufacture and materials used. Additionally, if you are importing products made with any amount of wood, the declaration requirements can be very cumbersome. Google the Lacey Act to get a more complete description of what may be necessary; there is also some more information on page 74 of this book.

Wherever you decide to get your products made, keep a few pieces from each order for your records and write the date made and date received on those samples. Sometimes a manufacturer makes small changes that you did not ask for; if you are not happy about it, you will need some back-up evidence. Have the manufacturer send you samples from the order before they ship the rest. When the bulk of the order arrives, make sure that you receive exactly the same thing as what you approved, and that the advance sample was not just a piece from a previous order.

A manufacturer once shipped us an acceptable sample, but when the new order arrived, it had a change that we hadn't asked for. We documented the discrepancy, and they had to make good on it. In that case, we accepted the order at a lower price.

When a change has been made without your approval, maybe a different tint or size, decide if it is absolutely necessary to correct it. It can take a relatively long time to remake and ship goods. While it would seem that the manufacturer should pick up all the costs of collecting the defects, remaking the order and reshipping, they will likely do everything they can to keep from having to take an order back.

Decide how bad the discrepancy is, and if your clients will notice or even care. If it is something made especially for a catalog, store or chain of stores, the client may refuse the order (or they may try to negotiate for a lower price, something you might be able to recoup from the manufacturer as a stipulation for keeping the goods). If it is for general distribution, as long as the change is not something that truly compromises the item, or makes it unsafe, you may be able to work out a great, new price with the manufacturer and just keep the stuff. We have done this on two occasions. But if it is clearly wrong, dangerous or unusable, do not accept the shipment. Fortunately, these types of inconsistencies have been the exception, not the rule. If you establish clear procedures and standards for your goods, it will remain the exception.

Where can you keep all of that stuff?

When your order arrives, you'll need to get it off the truck and into your facility. If it is on pallets you'll need a pallet jack or a forklift to move them. If you do not have a dock-high access to your place, you may need the goods delivered on a truck with a lift gate. In the beginning, we hand loaded boxes off of a 40' trailer and carried them into the warehouse. Over time we built an outside dock and installed roller conveyors. Though not motorized, it made it much easier to move the goods.

Imagine and role play all the steps that will happen from when the truck pulls up to when the stuff is stacked in storage. Delivery trucks sometimes charge for wait time. Be prepared.

Take Action!

▶ Decide early on where you are going to have your base of operations and if it has enough room to warehouse and ship your goods.

▶ Make sure your warehouse is safe, secure and accessible, with climate control if necessary.

▶ Keep accurate count of everything, and keep several samples from every shipment. Label samples with the order number and date received.

21. Oh no, not again! Look at the Time!

 Fishtip™: Plan ahead. Way way ahead.

Remember before when I said that in sales and marketing, and therefore in manufacturing and shipping, timing is everything? We just went over the manufacturing and shipping. Think about how many scheduling decisions are involved.

There's a reason the Fishtip™ above is in here twice.

Take Action!

▶ Visualize the whole scenario of designing and making, then receiving and shipping your orders. This is a great way to minimize surprises.

▶ Make sure everyone knows when you need to receive your goods so that you can fill orders: the factory, the shipper and your warehouse personnel.

▶ Decide what you will do if your perfectly laid plan goes awry. Remember, you are a problem solver and you want happy customers. They will appreciate a heads-up, proactive approach to stave off disaster.

▶ Since you are well prepared, plan that party to celebrate your successful efforts! Invite everyone who helped you. Enjoy!

> *"Even when you think you have your life all mapped out, things happen that shape your destiny in ways you might never have imagined."*
>
> ### Deepak Chopra
> *Medical Doctor and Writer, Focusing on Spirituality and Mind-Body Medicine*

Selling The Scream

22. Are you juggling one ball too many?

 Fishtip™: You are an Entrepreneur: make sure all hires know what that means. Explain the big picture so employees will know when opportunities present themselves. Encourage employees to think beyond their day-to-day duties.

 Fishtip™: Hire carefully! Give the process the time it needs.

 Fishtip™: Create an employee manual (outlines responsibilities) and an office manual (describes everything from where copier paper is to procedures for working with clients). Distribute the manuals, follow them and keep them updated.

 Fishtip™: Have two daily meetings, one to plan the day and establish what everyone expects to accomplish, then another at day's end to see what really did get done. If you work alone, have a meeting with yourself and make sure to Keep the Appointment!

 Fishtip™: Hold regularly scheduled employee evaluations and reviews.

OK, even though you can do everything yourself, you'll eventually need help. Not just advice. You'll need workers, either employees or contractors.

Any restaurant owner will tell you that hiring and keeping good staff is one of their biggest challenges. That's true of all businesses, from the smallest at-home cottage enterprise, to the largest multinational conglomerate.

Some help is available by partnering with companies (manufacturers, shippers, distributors), with individuals (your mentor, your personal banker), and with organizations (Better Business Bureau, local commerce and growth associations), and so on. But if your business grows, eventually you'll need hands-on help with the day-to-day details. If you don't get that help, you'll get overwhelmed and frustrated, and you won't have time for the fun stuff anymore. Like being innovative. Like evolving your *crazy idea* and developing new products and new marketing ideas. Like networking at B2B events.

If you're right-brained enough to have come up with a *crazy idea*, then probably day-to-day details feel like a bottomless pit. Hire somebody who thrives on detail-work and get out of their way! (If you're the detail-work type and you've made it this far with your *crazy idea*, you may want to partner with a "creative type" to balance out that side of your business.)

Usually the first place you'll need help is the office. Filing, making and receiving calls, bookkeeping, scheduling appointments and meetings, keeping things organized. These days, you may need a web master to help with your online presence. Eventually you'll want someone to be in charge of sales. Maybe this will be your job, maybe not.

I had a hard time finding and deciding on qualified help. I didn't want to spend much time on staffing issues, so I sped through the hiring process, and sometimes I kept people on long after a mismatch was obvious. In those cases, the employee and I were both unhappy, but I overlooked the gaps and hoped that 'things would work out."

Firing someone is personally awkward and a legal minefield, but keeping mismatched employees can cost you money (unemployment fees, legal costs), and hurt everyone's morale. It hurts the employee in the long run, too. Sure, that individual keeps getting paychecks, but he or she misses the chance to thrive as a worker.

Advertise for employees on places as diverse as coffee shop or college bulletin boards, stay at home Mom's in your school district's or community's newsletter, newspaper classifieds or websites like craigslist.com, Monster.com, careerbuilder.com or elance.com. Be very clear about job duties, expectations and compensation. Get resumés and study them; check recent references. If you are hiring recent college grads, ask their teachers about the grads' levels of commitment, responsibility, relevant knowledge and skill.

See if you feel comfortable with the candidate's personality and work habits, and them with you. Check with your state's employment guidelines; there is usually a 30-day grace period in which you can let someone go for no particular reason, without having to pay them unemployment.

In hiring people and growing a business, you are essentially creating multiples of yourself. You want your vision to be far-reaching and have an effect on people's lives…and you want to make money.

Involve your employees as much as possible. They will have more incentive to be personally invested in the business, thus partnering with you in achieving success. Create a work environment where they can think like entrepreneurs. Otherwise, you'll all be out of a job.

Hire carefully; then trust and manage your staff so your employees can manage their parts of your business. To do this, you must feel confident that they can do more than just take care of things, that they will also take initiative and see problems before they arise, and come up with workable, innovative solutions. The more responsibility you can give to an employee, the more that they can be in charge of, the more decisions they can make on your behalf, the better they will perform. If you decide to make a commitment to them that success is shared, they will have more at stake and will rise to the occasion to make you and themselves happy. Foster an atmosphere of inclusion, so they feel that their ideas and suggestions are valued. You absolutely do not want employees to fear expressing themselves: everyone loses when that happens

Don Goldman, president of Goldman Promotions in St. Louis, MO, took pride in the fact that he provided a livelihood for over 200 people, and thus, for their families as well. He took this responsibility very seriously and it figured into much of his decision-making. His attention to their well being was reciprocated by a high level of performance in all areas of the company. Don't be an absent leader. Everyone is looking to you for guidance and reassurance.

You may only need to hire people for specific jobs or short-term tasks. These people would be considered contractors, not employees, and are either paid hourly, like a web designer, or receive a set fee, like to build something for you. It is still important to lay out your expectations and have at least a simple contract. Talk with them about potential problems or delays. If they seem reluctant to discuss these matters, look for someone else. Make sure to get references and check them out for not just the quality of their work, but how they were to work with. You want work to be as pleasant and fun as possible, and you want to make money.

Take Action!

- ▶ Think about the scope of your *crazy idea* and if you will need paid help.

- ▶ Will you need staff or contractors?

- ▶ Identify the best place to look for help.

- ▶ What types of facilities and resources will you need to support the staff?

- ▶ Find someone to discuss the potential hires with; consider it a reality check.

- ▶ Be clear about who is responsible for what.

> *"In the early days, I didn't have the money to pay decent salaries, so I didn't get good people. I got nice people, but I didn't get good employees."*
>
> Louise Hay
> *Motivational Author*

> *"The buck stops with me, but I can tick off dozens of very good senior executives that are responsible for hundreds or thousands of people who work for me."*
>
> Rupert Murdoch
> *Australian born global media mogul*

Lindy Squared, our most well known mural: before, scraping, measuring, painting 1,200 squares with 72 shades of gray paint, the image emerging and finished!

This page from the top: Soulard Market, Que sera Seurat?, Face of a Nation, Car Heaven with inset detail. All painted in Saint Louis, all © ON THE WALL, and all now gone.

Over a period of ten years, while I sold *Screams*, my wife Sarah continued to create murals. These are a few she painted on a complex of buildings for Willert Home Products in St. Louis, making it a tourist destination. Located near 39th & Park In the city.

SINTRA®
Case History

"FINE ART CUT-OUTS" ARE A CUT ABOVE WITH SINTRA.

Artist Robert Fishbone, owner of On The Wall Productions, has found some pretty off the wall uses for Sintra Material in a variety of display and environmental art applications. His fine art cut-outs range from recreations of classics like Munch's Scream and Gauguin Tahitians to seven foot penguins and Arnold Palmer look-alikes. Such creative, detailed applications often entail cutting, painting and laminating Sintra Material for both indoor and outdoor use. Yet, according to Fishbone, in every instance, Sintra Material has never failed to perform beautifully.

ROBERT FISHBONE—ARTIST/OWNER, ON THE WALL PRODUCTIONS, INC., ST. LOUIS, MISSOURI:
"We call it the 'amazing Sintra.' It's lightweight, so it's easy to transport. Cuts like a dream, I can even cut backwards with the dull side of a blade if I need to. Its ultra-smooth finish allows for very detailed work and its edges never drop-out or show weathering. It is initially more expensive than other materials, and believe me, we've tried everything—Medex, Gatorboard, Masonite, Fome-Cor and MDO plywood. But all the advantages that Sintra Material offers make it the overall best value and our board of choice."

On The Wall's unique cut-outs have appeared nationwide and because they're always so well-received, are often displayed much longer than anticipated. Once again, Fishbone is quick to point out that incredible durability is yet another big advantage of using Sintra Material.

So no matter what you're creating, try Sintra Material. It's the lightweight, easy to fabricate, durable creative sheet material that can turn any project into a true work of art.

SINTRA®
MATERIAL

Photo above by Keeven Photography St. Louis, MO
Sintra Case History reprinted courtesy Alcan Composites USA, Inc

To market our painting abilities, we created a series of cut-outs of figures from famous paintings and from nature. We kept these in our offices as decorations and to impress clients. Everyone loved them, especially *The Scream*. The endless comments about how weird it was made me think there was something else we could do with it...but what?

Photo above by Keeven Photography, St. Louis, MO

Fishbone and the entire family of *Scream* products (above), a few pieces of international print media and some of the more than one hundred submissions mailed in to our online museum, the *Screameria*.

は話題を呼び、
ンマークからや
で、麻生健写す

SCREAM of WHEAT

A Good Source of Anxiety
in A very Healthy Food

DagensNæringsliv

Uke 5 — Mandag
27. januar 1992

Nr. 22 – Årg. 103
Løssalg kr. 15,00

Dagens Næringsliv   ETTER BØRS   Mandag 27. januar 1992 · 25

Skriket selger
så det griner

■ Kultur

Av HANS

sjon er blitt meget godt mottatt.
Den selger bra i USA, og har
også solgt bra i Australia, rap-
porterer Robert Fishbone, som

«Skriket» fra USA er blitt
solgt gjennom venner og venners
venner, men nå er Robert
Fishbone i ferd med å finne for-
som ønsker å selge
blåsbare versjonen av
Munchs udødelige og
mest kjente motiv.
hevder å ha loven på sin
ns Munch-museet argu-
med at gjengivelsen er
lansert, daglig mottar
Fishbone brev om hva de
ge kundene bruker
berømmet til.
ror «Skriket» vil holde
arkedet i flere år, at vår
ker noe mer enn en dagn-

shape is good and the
is nice, sier Robert

WE'RE
DOOMED

Even though the *Scream* line continued to sell well, my stores and my staff wanted us to start making something else. After a good deal of discussion we added the Scream's long lost cousin, the Little Happy Guy. They were both a hit in the Clinton White House.

We also added a line of Egyptian merchandise because Egypt is Eternal! We made an inflatable sarcopogus in two sizes based on the one at the St. Louis Art Museum, as well as two coffee mugs, two keychains, an iconic beachball (below) and a children's art activity, "Draw Like an Egyptian".

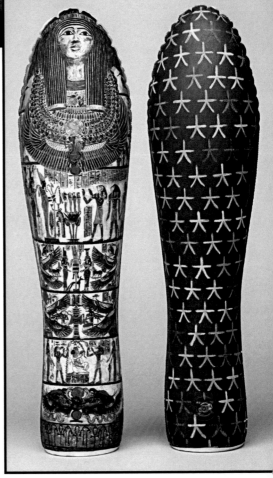

All photo's this page and following two pages by Keeven Photography, St. Louis

Our very popular, and twice despised game, *Pin The Ear on Van Gogh* in action. Sold with 10 numbered ears using Post it™ adhesive and instructions in eight languages, English, French, Spanish, German, Dutch, Swedish, Italian, and Japanese, it is based on a birthday party game my wife made for me. She recreated a Van Gogh self portrait (right) and then made up the bottom half with 'Sunflowers', as well as the 'Starry Night' sky. We sold about 25,000 of them.

Dali Clocks

Above: The jinxed clocks we made based on Salvador Dali's painting, *"The Persistance of Memory."* See the chapter entitled $297,372.61 to read about how my stupid decision to pursue this project almost ruined us.

Facing page: A new line of products we developed from a promotional item called a Magic Cube helped pull us out of the hole. Ironically, the Dali Cube we made for the Salvador Dali Museum in St. Petersburg, FL was one of the our most popular designs. In addition to the forty designs we created for in house use by a wide variety of clients, we grew the wholesale line to over fifty titles. We worked hard to establish relationships with very prestigious clients like the Metropolitan Museum in New York, the Smithsonian Institute, the Art Institute of Chicago, Andy Warhol Foundation for the Visual Arts, NASA / Jet Propulsion Lab and Lockheed Martin Company.

Between the Magic Cubes and a line of musical instruments I developed (last color page), I was able to grow my company into a profitable entity once again. And it was at that point that I sold the Magic Cubes and retired from the world of product to enter the world of Professional Speaking.

Magic Cubes

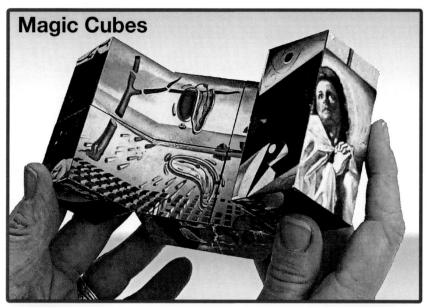

Thunder Tube

Amazing sound effects device

Thunder Tubes™ & Washboard Ties™: Like with the Magic Cubes, I have taken two other existing products and reinvented their identities, making them appeal to wider audiences than their original designs. The Washboard Tie™, formerly the Zydeco Tie™ invented by Laura Geisen, comes with two thimbles so you can have an instant party. Looks cool, plays hot!

Remo Belli, the founder of Remo, Inc. was impressed by my ability to sell odd products to a variety of market niches. He challenged me to do something with their Spring Drums which I re-invented as Thunder Tubes™. Their simplicity and low price point, along with their ability to generate an entire pallette of sound effects gives them a very wide appeal.

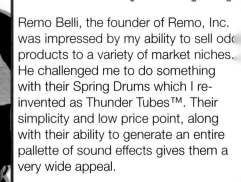

Dealing with Problems

Everything will go smoothly with your *crazy idea*, and you'll live happily ever after.

But just in case....

23. How do you spell SUED?

 Fishtip™: Do your legal homework.

 Fishtip™: When resolving conflicts, keep at it until you reach a mutually beneficial solution.

We nearly got sued, and we ended up in a morass of international legal entanglements. You will likely not get trapped in that same situation, but if reading our story simply impresses on you the importance of doing your legal homework – whatever it may be – then it's worth your time. Here we go.

Before we began manufacturing our *Scream* inflatable, I got some advice on the copyright status of Edvard Munch's painting, *"The Scream,"* which inspired our inflatables. Staff at **Volunteer Lawyers for the Arts** assured me that the painting was in the public domain. US Copyright law has gone through many changes, but one base guideline is that any work published before January 1, 1923 anywhere in the world is in the public domain in the United States. For an artwork, publishing means it just needs to be reproduced somewhere, such as in a magazine or book, on a poster advertising a show, or actually exhibited in a show. Being in the public domain means anyone can now copy, reproduce, modify, parody or otherwise use it in any way they want and for any purpose. Proper attribution to the author or source of a work, even if it is in the public domain, is still required to avoid plagiarism, though not everyone abides by this convention.

OK, so we were good to go. We started selling in 1991 and sales quickly took off. More and more stores and catalogs were selling them in large numbers (20,000 pieces our first full year) and we were frankly stunned by the sudden success. I was working my butt off to fill orders. Our friends at ACME were also pleased (and relieved) that we were able to not just keep buying the inventory they were holding for us, but begin to place factory re-orders. We even began selling some in Europe.

Then two events changed our business. First, The winter Olympics were being held Norway, home of *"The Scream"* painting, so there were hundreds of thousands of sports fans and journalists from all over the world enjoying the spectacle in person. While all attention was focused on the Games, thieves leaned a ladder against the National Gallery in downtown Oslo one night, broke some windows, climbed through and stole *"The Scream."** The thieves even left a note that said, "Thanks for the poor security."

> *A different version is owned and exhibited at the Munch Museum in another part of the city, and that one was actually stolen several years later! What is it with this painting? Both paintings have since been recovered.*

It also happened that a number of people were walking around the slopes carrying our 54" inflatable *Scream*, with the figures appropriately dressed for the winter with woolen ski hats and scarves. The day after the painting was stolen, five thousand journalists then swung their cameras towards not just the National Gallery, but towards our product and asked, "So what's the deal with *The Scream?*" meaning the inflatables and the missing artwork. Since our company name and address were on the product (an obvious but sometimes overlooked marketing tactic), I got phone calls and faxes from all over the world, especially in Japan. The Japanese magazine, *Friday*, their equivalent of *Time* or *Newsweek*, did a big article on me when I visited Japan later that year. Amazing free publicity. It was a fine time.

Not only did our sales dramatically increase, but people started interviewing me as an expert in the pop icon status of *"The Scream."* It didn't stop there, though. Some thought things were too coincidental and flat-out asked, "Did *you* steal it?" No! But it did wonders for our bottom line.

Then that second thing happened…. **DACS, the Design and Artists Copyright Society**, caught wind of our sales in the UK. It turns out that *"The Scream"* was still protected, really well protected, by copyright laws outside of the US. Though the artwork was in the public domain in the US, it was still copyright protected everyplace else in the world. In Norway the rule is "death of the artist plus 70 years." Since Edvard Munch, who painted *"The Scream,"* died in 1944, the work will be protected through 2014.

Busted!

Dagens Næringsliv

HUNT FOR "THE SCREAM"

May, 1994
By Hans Hjellemo

*Reprinted with permission
of Hans Hjellemo and
Dagens Næringsliv*

Edvard Munch's heirs and the Munch Museum in Oslo have now started the hunt for the American inflatable version of Edvard Munch's famous motif "The Scream". The goal is to stop production and sale of the product in the U.S., England and Germany. At the same time, Tronsmo bookstore in Oslo has started over-the-counter sales of the 180 cm tall "Scream', which has been the store's most popular product since Easter.

The highly original interpretation of Munch's most famous motif, "The Scream", first found its way to Norway two years ago. By that time, Robert Fishbone of the American company On The Wall Productions in the U.S. had long been shipping "The Scream" all over the U.S. and exporting it to a number of European countries. When Dagens Næringsliv first wrote about the case in 1992, Alf Bøe, president of the Munch Museum, literally reacted with a scream.

Robert Fishbone had not obtained permission from Munch's heirs or paid royalties on the sale. However, legal experts determined that the American was free to produce and sell the product in the U.S., where copyright laws are based on the art work's copyright and year of publication, matters to which Munch himself did not pay much attention. In Norway, on the other hand, any sale of the product is illegal.

Most Popular Sales Item
The Tronsmo bookstore has completely missed the point.

"We have been selling the Americans' popular version of "The Scream" over the counter since Easter. In this short period of time, the product has, undoubtedly, become our best-selling item. We've been selling in good faith, without realizing that this is illegal

How do you spell SUED?

97

according to Norwegian copyright laws," says Manager Anne Ti-
tlestad at the Tronsmo bookstore in Oslo to Dagens Næringsliv.

She tells us that the bookstore discovered the product via a mail-
order company, and that they bought one sample to exhibit in
the window. As time went by, demand became so great that they
started to import directly from Robert Fishbone's company.

Robert Fishbone has had the most success selling to psychiatrists,
who ordered the plastic version for their offices.

Pursues the Case
One of the reasons that it has taken so much time to pursue the
two-year-old case, is that an agreement between the Oslo Mu-
nicipality, the Munch Museum and Munch's heirs to transfer the
administration of Munch's copyright to BONO was not concluded
until last fall. The agreement has now been renewed and is valid
until August of this year.

"We have obtained all authorizations to pursue this case both in the
U.S. and Europe, with the goal of stopping production as well as
distribution of the product. From now on, the case has been given
top priority, and a few weeks ago we contacted our sister organiza-
tions in the U.S., England and Germany in order to possibly pros-
ecute the case," says Harald Holter, manager of BONO, to Dagens
Næringsliv.

We have also contacted the manufacturer in an attempt to stop the
product on a moral basis. Besides, we were recently informed that
"The Scream" is being sold in Oslo. Before we take any measures
vis-à-vis the Tronsmo bookstore, we are waiting to see how our
sister organizations in England, Germany and the U.S. view this
case from a legal perspective," says Holtere.

Extended Protection Period
In Norway, the protection period for Munch's pictures is valid until
the year 2000. If, however, the proposal by the Ministry of Culture
for a new and revised intellectual property law goes into effect, the
Munch Museum expects the copyrights for Edvard Munch will not
expire until the year 2014. The Ministry of Culture will present a
new law this spring, but Parliament will probably not consider it until

next session.

Edvard Munch's original "Scream" was recently stolen from the National Gallery. If the National Gallery wants an inflatable replacement it better act quickly, before the sale of "The Scream" becomes history at the Tronsmo bookstore as well.

◉   ◉   ◉

DACS halted the sales of our products in the UK, Germany and Norway and began sending threatening faxes (no emails yet). It didn't help that the Munch Museum despised our 'plastic dolls.' I didn't know what to do; it was an awful, awful time. Every day I would go downstairs to my home office and see some new communication from Solicitors (lawyer-types in the UK) saying what would happen if I didn't stop selling.

An intellectual property lawyer advised me to try and reach a settlement – fantastic advice and well worth his fee. I convinced DACS, and thus the **Munch Estate**, that they actually had a lot to gain by granting us a worldwide license to sell our products. I offered that if they granted us a worldwide license, I would include all US sales in the agreement to pay them royalties. This was very generous of me as by far the bulk of sales were in the US, where we were under no obligation to pay royalties. But I could see that including US sales in the Agreement would seal the deal.

It felt like a miracle, and maybe it was – a miracle based on a LOT of hard work: we worked out a **Worldwide Licensing Agreement** that included paying a certain amount of restitution on past sales as well as a royalty on future sales. Soon, we were legally selling our *Scream* products all over the world. It worked out well for all parties. It was fine times again.

What does this have to do with your *crazy idea*? Do your legal homework, especially if artworks or other types of intellectual property are involved. While the original work may be in the public domain, it is highly likely that reproductions of it in any other media have a separate, new and still valid copyright. The Internet unfortunately gives the illusion that this is a blurry issue…it usually is not.

How do you spell SUED?   99

Just look at the legal dispute that went on shortly after Barack Obama was elected President of the United States. Artist Shepard Fairey surfed the web and found a photo of Obama, shot by a photographer contracted by the Associated Press (AP). Fairey used the photo to create a red, white and blue "head shot" poster that has now become an icon. On February 4, 2009 the AP said that use of the photograph requires its permission and entered negotiations with Fairey's attorney. However, the artist then filed a pre-emptive suit against AP, saying he had **Fair Use** on his side. AP has counter-sued claiming copyright infringement and that Fairey's work was clearly a derivative of the original. Then the photographer said he owned the rights and was thrilled and perfectly happy with how it was used; though he also implied that if he could be paid, he wouldn't object. Do you want to be in the middle of something like that? Probably not.

We hate those plastic dolls!

The Munch Museum refused to carry our products, or as they put it, "the offending parodies." They did not buy my argument that we were actually making the artwork better known and more popular (we always placed information about the original painting on our packaging.)

Their refusal to sell our products even after signing off on the Licensing Agreement went on for a year or two. Then, with a change in museum personnel, they decided to sell our goods in their shop. They created an area especially for parodies, thus making a distinction from true reproductions of the artwork. It worked out well for all parties concerned, and no one ended up suing anybody.

There is often a simple and clear, mutually beneficial solution hiding somewhere within the complexities of the situation. Lead with your positive attitude, show humility and grace, admit your mistakes, don't get too defensive or aggressive, get good legal advice, be clear in your own mind about what you want before communicating and then state what it is you want. Keep it simple and learn to bend like a reed.

Take Action!

▶ Check the legal status of your "property." Then check it again. Maybe even one more time. Then have someone else review and confirm your research.

▶ If you get involved in a legal dispute, hire a lawyer. Ask and understand how they will charge you for their time and expenses. Remain calm: nothing is decided until it is decided.

▶ Read the next chapter to see what type of intellectual property protection might be available for your *crazy idea*.

▶ Important: If you are not already familiar with the **Orphan Works Act of 2008**, now is the time to start reading up on it. See Glossary for more information.

Selling The Scream

24. Are *you* breaking any laws?

 Fishtip™: Make sure your product does not violate import or safety laws. Be aware of cultural sensitivities.

 Fishtip™: Testing your product, especially something marketed to children, can cost more than you will make. Research this!

There are multiple facets of this question: legal issues, manufacturing issues and social/cultural issues.

Legal issues

You just read about how we got busted for breaking international copyright law. There are also the matters of patent protection and trademarks to consider, many of which are country-specific. All add some protection to your creations. Thoroughly research the chance that your crazy new idea is not so now and may be competing with someone else's. If it turns out that there's a competitor with an unprotected idea, then it's just a question of duking it out in the marketplace. If you find that your idea is already protected, you can try to negotiate a deal with the original owner of the idea, or just fuggeddabowdit and do something else. Legal problems can go on forever and cost all the money in the world.

If your idea is original and you want to pursue it, look into which type of protection would best suit your venture. Start with the following definitions from **wikipedia.org** (September 1, 2008), but don't stop there. Seek legal help to understand and secure the right protections.

Copyright* is a legal concept, enacted by governments, giving the creator of an original work of authorship exclusive rights to it, usually for a limited time, after which the work enters the public domain. Generally, it is "the right to copy", but usually provides the author with other rights as well, such as the right to be credited for the work, to determine who may adapt the work to other forms, who may perform the work, who may financially benefit from it, and other, related rights. It is an intellectual property form (like the patent, the trademark, and the trade secret) applicable to any expressible form of an idea or information that is substantive and discrete.

Copyright was initially conceived as a way for governments in Europe to restrict printing; the contemporary intent of copyright is to promote the creation of new works by giving authors control of and profit from them.

Copyright has been internationally standardized, lasting between fifty to a hundred years from the author's death, or a finite period for anonymous or corporate authorship; some jurisdictions have required formalities to establishing copyright, most recognize copyright in any completed work, without formal registration.

Most jurisdictions recognize copyright limitations, allowing "fair" exceptions to the author's exclusivity of copyright, and giving users certain rights. The development of the Internet, digital media, computer network technologies, such as peer-to-peer filesharing, have prompted reinterpretation of these exceptions, introduced new difficulties in enforcing copyright, and inspired additional challenges to copyright law's philosophic basis. Simultaneously, businesses with great economic dependence upon copyright have advocated the extension and expansion of their copyrights, and sought additional legal and technological enforcement.

A **Patent*** is a set of exclusive rights granted by a state (meaning country) to an inventor or his assignee for a fixed period of time in exchange for a disclosure of an invention.

The procedure for granting patents, the requirements placed on the patentee and the extent of the exclusive rights vary widely between countries according to national laws and international agreements. Typically, however, a patent application must include one or more claims defining the invention which must be new, inventive, and useful or industrially applicable. In many countries, certain subject areas are excluded from patents, such as business methods and mental acts. The exclusive right granted to a patentee in most countries is the right to prevent or exclude others from making, using, selling, offering to sell or importing the invention.

A **Trademark*** or **Trade Mark** (represented by the symbol ™) or **Mark** is a distinctive sign or indicator of some kind which is used by an individual, business organization or other legal entity to identify uniquely the source of its products and/or services to consumers and to distinguish its products or services from those of other entities. A trademark is a type of intellectual property and typically a name, word, phrase, logo, symbol, design, image, or a combination of these elements. There is also a range of non-conventional trademarks comprising marks which do not fall into these standard categories.

The owner of a registered trademark may commence legal proceedings for trademark infringement to prevent unauthorized use of that trademark. However, registration is not required. The owner of a common law trademark may also file suit, but an unregistered mark may be protect-able only within the geographical area within which it has been used or in geographical areas into which it may be reasonably expected to expand.

Manufacturing Restrictions

People and countries worldwide have become much more sensitive and careful about the use of protected resources in the manufacturing of, as well as safety issues related to those products. Two current examples:

1) All wood products imported into the US now need to be labeled with the type of wood, plus where it came from, when it was harvested, where and how it was processed and manufactured. While there is justification for these laws, imagine the extra burden this puts, for instance, on cottage musical instrument manufacturers.

2) We've all heard about lead paint on toys. Lead and certain other materials are becoming highly restricted or outright banned on most products, especially toys. Again, justifiable, but very tricky. If you send a design to China for a wooden toy, it may be worked on by several suppliers and manufacturers. Try tracking the ingredients in every part! Plastics are under great scrutiny these days. Do your homework and write careful, detailed contracts. Stay up to date on all of these rules and laws or you could end up with a warehouse full of un-sellable products. Start with the US Department of Commerce for the latest guidelines on import restrictions.

Are you breaking any laws? 105

Case in point: Trophy Music, the distributor for my line of novelty percussion instruments, sells many other related items. Under the new laws, they have to test every component of every instrument. For a children's guitar that means each different type of wood, the strings, all plastic parts, and coating or sealers on the wood or metal parts such as the tuners and even the logo that is printed on the guitar. In fact, there is so little ink in the logo that they were asked to send in 50 samples so the tester could scrape off enough ink to test!

Testing your product, especially something marketed to children, can cost more than you will make. Research this!

Cultural or Social Restrictions

This is a gray area. Something that is seen as harmless or funny in one culture may be viewed as very offensive in another. Research the product through the Internet and respectfully talk with someone from the cultures where you are thinking of marketing your product.

Find someone with an open and understanding mindset. Like translations that take on a very different meaning, you also need to be careful when explaining your product in another country. The last thing you want to do is offend. This can result in more than just a lost marketing opportunity: remember what happened when cartoons about Islam appeared in Danish newspapers? There were demonstrations and even riots in countries around the world by people who took great offense to the images and accompanying text.

Take Action!

▶ Determine which type of protection will work best for you. Work with a lawyer. Remember that copyrights, patents and trademarks all have the potential of resale value.

▶ Make sure you know what current safety laws will apply to your product.

▶ If you are going to sell overseas, speak with people from that culture to make sure your *crazy idea* will be appreciated, not vilified.

Naming Your Product for Overseas Sale

In China, the name Coca-Cola was first rendered as Ke-kou-ke-la. Unfortunately, the Coke company did not discover until after thousands of signs had been printed that the phrase means "bite the wax tadpole" or "female horse stuffed with wax." Coke then researched 40,000 Chinese characters and found a close phonetic equivalent, ko-kou-ko-le, which can be loosely translated as "happiness in the mouth."

When translated into Chinese, the Kentucky Fried Chicken slogan "finger-lickin' good" came out as "eat your fingers off."

Colgate introduced a toothpaste in France called Cue, the name of a notorious porno magazine.

In Italy, a campaign for Schweppes Tonic Water translated the name into Schweppes Toilet Water.

When Parker Pen marketed a ball-point pen in Mexico, its ads were supposed to say "It won't leak in your pocket and embarrass you." However, the "translator" thought the Spanish word "embarazar" meant embarrass...wrong! So the ads said that "It won't leak in your pocket and make you pregnant."

*Wikipedia Citations :
http://en.wikipedia.org/wiki/Copyright, September 1, 2008
http://en.wikipedia.org/wiki/Trademark, September 1, 2008
http://en.wikipedia.org/wiki/Patent, September 1, 2008

25. "What else do you have?"

 Fishtip™: "One hit wonders" rarely survive.

 Fishtip™: Stores would rather sell a line than a single product. They know that choice drives sales.

 Fishtip™: Make a plan for success.

OK, your first product as an entrepreneur was a success, and not just a monetary success: You've gotten great publicity in the national and international Press. You've resolved potentially disastrous legal issues. You are acquiring more and more outlets for your product, you are riding high. You are a genius and anything you do will be a success.

You have The Golden Touch.

And then one of your best accounts asks, "What else do you have?"

Planning for Success

Though I touch on this briefly in other places in this book, I want to address the Problem of Success. Most people plan for things going wrong, for disaster, for unforeseen circumstances wrecking havoc on your well thought out *crazy idea*...smart. And it would be equally wise to prepare for success.

What will you do if you make a LOT of money? Hire more staff? Get a larger facility?

Get a nicer facility? Fill up your glorious new offices with furnishings befitting a successful business? Grow your line? License other properties? Give your employees bonuses? Live the high life, maybe travel overseas? Buy a new home?

But what about taxes on all of that new income, or managing all of those new hires? How about paying guaranteed royalties on that licensed property, getting more insurance to cover your expanded operation and larger inventory, or being locked into a multi year lease? Maybe your time is no longer your own and you are traveling all the time, for business, and you can't enjoy that new home and those lovely offices.

And what happens if in a year, for unforeseen reasons, things don't continue to go your way, and you need to scale back? What obligations would you be stuck with? Would you still be able to maintain your bigger business? How about loan repayments? These are not just what-ifs, these are things that really happen.

A business plan needs to have contingencies for ups and downs, and it needs to be flexible. You have to review it and make sure it is still relevant to your evolving circumstances. Remember what I said earlier: *Think of your business plan as a map. A map doesn't make you go anywhere, but it helps you make decisions about which way to turn, and it lets you check to make sure you're headed toward your destination.*

"What else? What do you mean?"

"What else do you sell? Your first product is great but most products run out of steam eventually so you'll need something else to takes its place…or at least give customers a choice. So what else do you have?"

How you deal with this will make a huge difference in everything else that follows.

Sure, maybe your first idea will last forever and you can retire, but most likely, not.

So, are you going to grow that same line? Or start something else? Maybe you need to decide not just where you want your business to go but also your life. What's your plan?

For us, the scattershot approach worked fine for several years (except for that copyright glitch). We had a wildly popular product embraced by the media and sold in stores and catalogs in 15 countries. Big bucks were coming in.

After careful consideration, I made an important decision to adjust my original business plan: Now, I'll Make *More* Stuff and Sell it!

Invent an entirely different product or make variations on the proven? I went for variations, and I'd recommend it first. It's easier and less risky. See how you can vary what you have, rather than starting the invention process over again.

We made *Scream* inflatables in other sizes, then as keychains, mugs, mousepads and T-shirts. We gave customers choices; instead of deciding whether to buy a *Scream*, they would be deciding *which Scream* to buy.

Though we were doing just fine with the expanded *Scream* line, my wife and staff started grumbling; they wanted to develop other themes. "Couldn't we do something else, something that's not so, like, tormented?"

After listening to their ideas for a couple of months, I decided to listen to my own advice and gave them the responsibility for new product development: their assignment was to draft a list of well thought out suggestions to also include packaging concepts and target markets. The result? A bunch of great new ideas! Our next product was based on a party game that my wife had put together for my birthday the previous year: *Pin the Ear on Van Gogh*. Knowing it would achieve international success it came with instructions in eight languages. The 'game board' was a beautiful large poster based on my wife's painting, in and of itself worth the selling price. It had 10 numbered ears with Post-It® adhesive so you could play it over and over without having to keep making holes with pins. It was a hit and we sold about 25,000 pieces.

Then we went Egyptian, and made a 60" and 20" inflatable sarcophagus based on the one at the St. Louis Art Museum. We also made two keychains, and two mugs, all with 'Egyptian themes. These all sold well, though not as well as the *Scream* stuff....about 50,000 of the mummies.

Then we made the *Scream*, Jr's alter ego, the Little Happy Guy. Using the same body mold as the 20" *Scream* inflatable, it had a round, happy smiling face and outstretched arms. Colored a very bright yellow, it just wanted to give you a big fat hug. Some customers bought a *Scream*, Jr and a Little Happy Guy to use as mood indicators on their desks:

"You May Approach / Stay Away!"

Since we already had a large and diverse client base around the world, we were able to offer these to existing clients while at the same time expanding to untapped markets with the new subject matter.

Wow, this is Fun!

Each success came, though, with its own unexpected...surprise. For example, some people wanted us to stop selling the Van Gogh game because they felt it made fun of someone with mental disease. There was even one short article about this in the *New York Times*, which of course just increased demand, which led to better sales. Some stores wanted to keep carrying it, so they began selling it from under the counter – literally. You had to know they had it and ask. You had to do the secret handshake, too, before the store admitted they had any.

Take Action!

▶ Go to a store and look at the variety in any product category. How are different people trying to make their product stand out? Are they offering a choice?

▶ See how many different ways you can vary your *crazy idea*.

▶ For fun, take someone else's *crazy idea* and do the same thing. Does that give you any new ideas that you could legally and ethically introduce?

> *"Every time a man (or woman) puts a new idea across he finds ten men who thought of it before he did-but they only thought of it."*
>
> Anonymous

From The Screameria:

Dear *Scream*:

I would like to know if I can get the *Scream* Jr. inflatable anywhere. I am an English teacher & I used it in my classroom. Sometimes I had it holding my bathroom pass. For some reason it kept the pass from getting lost as easily as it usually does. The kids seemed to like to place it in the *Scream's* arms. Yes, notice the sadness of the use of the past tense. One day, a couple of weeks ago, the students were in a group & *Scream* had fallen on the floor & Marco picked it up, but instead of just replacing it, he acted like a 14 year old, which he is, & tried to bop Mohanish, a much taller boy, on the head. Mohanish tried to brush the attack of little Marco off, perceiving him to be a little gnat, & in the process, *Scream's* head somehow got squeezed like a zit. I continue to tell them to stop acting acting their age, #@!/#!. So, the upshot is that I need a new *Scream* Jr. We all do miss it so. If you have any info, please let me know. Thanks.

☺   ☺   ☺

From Nancy Z:

We've had a large *Scream* in our front hall by our front door (which is glass) for years. Recently, our daughter amputated his arm by mistake. We have missed him terribly and are relieved to know that a replacement is on the way!

26. Keeping it Fresh

 Fishtip™: Exercise your mental muscles by fooling them.

 Fishtip™: Have fun with what you do at least once a day.

 Fishtip™: Look at your original list of *crazy ideas* and see if any others strike you as potential blockbusters.

If you get bored, your business will become boring. You will find yourself stuck, and you will lose – personally and professionally.

In any work situation, especially as an entrepreneur, the challenge is to keep it fresh.

Get some help. Get advice, or if you don't have one yet, consider getting a business partner or advisor. Perhaps they can take over the nuts and bolts stuff so you can get back to what you love, the excitement of the *crazy Idea*! The possibility of things, the potential of things…looking for and finding novel solutions to problems…

Read. There are a lot of books out there, as well as websites with tips on creativity (see Resources). They can provide many possibilities on ways to get unstuck. Try out a few techniques until you find some that work for you. Blend the keeper ideas into your daily routine.

Change something. Begin simply. Start with changing your office, or your routine. Even facing your chair in a different direction will work magic. At meetings, sit in different places. Wear different clothes. Start and stop work at different times. Your brain will wake up due to the rupturing of the routine; relationships change, your senses get reprogrammed and, from seeing things literally differently, you will have new ideas; guaranteed.

The furniture-moving and seat swapping taps into **Fung Shui**, an ancient Chinese system of plugging into positive life energy to improve one's life. Fung Shui often relates to light, and the direction and placement of furniture, mirrors, and windows in one's home or office. Changing your routines during meetings changes interpersonal dynamics, too. Just physically stirring things up can put staff on a more equal footing. That can promote more risk taking, which translates into new insights:

"I never noticed…"
"Wow, look at that…"
"What if we…"

Just like in sports, you must look for ways to cross train your mental muscles. I vary the kind of music I listen to, and I don't mean just put your MP3 player's same old stuff on shuffle. Mix folk, rap, classical, world, opera, rock, blues, hiphop, R&B and then put all that on shuffle. Listen to a friend's song mix. You'll rattle your thinking process and conjure fresh ideas and perspectives.

Do newspaper puzzles: sudoku, crossword, word jumbles, those quirky quotes that use letter substitution. They'll get your mind working in new ways….and, added benefit, some say these mental exercises delay or divert dementia.

Brushing your teeth with your other hand. Stepping up on a curb or stair with your other foot. Breaking habits produces new insights.

Figure out what kind of learner you are, and look for ways to take advantage of that tendency. I'm a kinesthetic learner (remember Gardner's Theory of Multiple Intelligences); movement helps me learn and remember. Dancers, most of whom are kinesthetic learners, learn things that have any kind of movement much faster than anyone else. They integrate their whole bodies into the experience, so they have a lot more computing and storage capacity at work than just their brain.

I try to learn like a dancer when I rehearse for story performances or speeches. I practice while I walk around the block. I also sweep the floor. You are putting your normal work methodology aside. The repetitive side-to-side motion is like Tai Chi, a moving form of meditation. Things slow down, You become humble. There is only the sound of your footsteps and the broom swishing back and forth. You start noticing tiny details of the room. Your whole sense of awareness is heightened. You accomplish something: the floor is clean.

We've all had the experience of getting up and walking around to think something out; this is usually accompanied by speaking out loud…it really helps, doesn't it? Don't be shy about adding movement and verbalizing to your thought process. In short, use as many senses as possible when working on the solution to a problem.

Have an activity every day that has a clearly defined goal. Sweeping a floor is like that: the floor was dirty and now it is clean. For exercise, I like weight lifting and rock climbing; it is clear when you have attained your goal and in the process you are totally focused, the rest of the world fades away.

Even the smallest of ideas for keeping things fresh will help things out, and may bring major breakthroughs.

On a global scale, remember that an innovative spirit is one of America's greatest strengths. Every work environment should foster creative thinking, and every worker should be looking for new ways of doing things. The price paid for being stale is failure.

Take Action!

- ▶ Go to www.animusic.com and look at *Pipe Dreams*. This will bend your brain in many ways and put a smile on your face.

- ▶ Take a ten-minute walk outside everyday with the purpose of solving some problem. Spend a minute afterwards recording your revelations. Review your notes the next day.

- ▶ Read "Extreme Creativity" in "The Future" section of this book

- ▶ Look at the next page and delve into the mysteries of Secret #5.

"It is a miracle that curiosity
survives formal education."

Albert Einstein
Physicist and Pacifist

"The most beautiful thing we can experience
is the mysterious. It is the source of all true
art and science."

Albert Einstein
Physicist and Pacifist

"Silence is the great teacher, and to learn its
lessons you must pay attention to it. There is
no substitute for the creative inspiration,
knowledge, and stability that come from knowing
how to contact your core of inner silence."

Deepak Chopra
*Medical Doctor and Writer, Focusing
on Spirituality & Mind-Body Medicine*

Secret #5
Balance creative play and business tasks.

There will always be a lot of nuts and bolts business stuff to do, that is guaranteed. But if you don't get enjoyment from what you do, if you don't take time to play, neither you nor your business will stay fresh, and you'll lose the innovative edge that is so important to your success. Just be sure you keep a balance…. Either get a partner who'll do all those nuts and bolts tasks for you, or, if you do it, use your positive attitude and careful, time management to make play time for yourself. Write some unstructured time into your business calendar….creativity and enjoyment are not just for nights, weekends or holidays.

Take Action!

- ▶ If you are doing everything yourself, think seriously about partnering. A veil will be lifted from your eyes and you'll stand straighter.

- ▶ Have a 15 minute recess period every day. If you have a staff, do something fun together…let it be a total escape.

- ▶ Go to a movie in the middle of the day.

- ▶ If you have any, bring your kids to work once in a while. They'll turn your serious business into a play room. Try and see what they see, it may freshen up your day, and the mess will not be all that hard to clean up. Maybe even use it as an opportunity to rearrange the office. Don't have kids? Borrow some… you'll also endear yourself to their parents.

> *"A business has to be involving, it has to be fun, and it has to exercise your creative instincts."*

Richard Branson
English industrialist, best known for his Virgin brand of over 360 companies

> *"I like to build things, I like to do things. I am having a lot of fun."*

Walter Chrysler
Machinist, railroad man and Founder of the Chrysler Corporation

> *"I could never be a politician because I think I'm too selfish, and I think I like to have fun.. the right to be irresponsible is a right I hold dear."*

Bono
Musician and activist

27. What's your business plan now Mr. or Ms. Smarty Pants?

 Fishtip™: Have a back-up plan for when (not if) disaster strikes.

With all of this in mind: the value of a plan, maintaining a balance between the creative and the practical, looking for ways to be more efficient, yet still be able to focus on innovation, I finally decided to make a major adjustment to my original plan. It would be a risky change. Now I was going to:

Make *Even More* Stuff and Sell it!

We followed the Happy Guy with inflatable, Glow in the Dark Gargoyles based on the ones at Notre Dame in Paris; amazing and way too expensive beach balls with textile graphics from cultures around the world; inflatable suns, moons, fish, fishbones (OK, a bow to my vanity), the *Venus of Willendorf* keychain…

Then I decided to do a clock which led to my worst business decision ever. My golden touch was an illusion. My BIG, wrong decision, was a reality.

Take Action!

▶ Use themes to expand your line. Make lists of the possibilities.

▶ Keep doing market research and marketing: is anyone really going to want to buy this new stuff? Call and check with your existing clients…use them as a versatile resource.

▶ Review your successes and failures: what are you learning? Put it into practice so you don't repeat mistakes.

▶ Ask for advice and get frequent reality checks. It's too easy to be seduced by success or to minimize lessons learned from failures.

▶ Look at the media and your competition as a way to follow trends in the marketplace.

From The Screameria:

In Pittsburgh, PA a family keeps a *Scream*, Jr. in the kids' room. It's called the "Ooo Guy" and it is there to protect the kids. After three years of over-ooing, the totem began to leak. So they called up and rush ordered another lest some tragedy befall the brood.

◉ ◉ ◉

When the *New York Times* wrote about my success selling the *Scream* inflatable, other publications followed. As they would shoot pictures, I already knew the shot that would work best, the one that they wanted but felt embarrassed to ask for. This was most apparent when I visited Japan on a *Scream* tour. Japan's Newsweek equivalent was doing a piece entitled "*Scream* is BIG in Japan." Being Japanese, they were very polite. But I knew that they wanted me to pose like the figure in the painting, hands to the sides of my head, mouth open. After about two dozen shots I said, "What do you think if I did this?" and struck the iconic pose. They smiled, clapped their hands together, said "Yes, yes yes!"...and that's the shot they put in. This probably occurred 30 times over a few years. It helps to know what the media needs.

28. $297,372.61

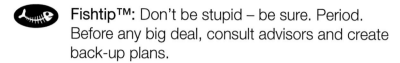 Fishtip™: Don't be stupid – be sure. Period. Before any big deal, consult advisors and create back-up plans.

Fishtip™: For big deals, get written, enforceable Purchase Orders beforehand.

Fishtip™: Remember your niche and do market research within your niche.

Fishtip™: Set price points that the market will bear and that are in keeping with your other products.

Fishtip™: There's no shame in bailing out when necessary: cut your losses.

Fishtip™: Avoid known legal complications. Compromise – or bail out.

$297,372.61. That's how much I lost through stupid decisions on a single product. There were warning signs along the way; when I look back, I can't believe that I pursued the project for two years, then paid for it for five.

I wanted to make a clock based on the melting clocks in Salvador Dali's painting, *"The Persistence of Memory."* Make our clock out of latex so it would actually bend as it spilled over a tabletop. How cool would that be?

Coincidentally, a friend of Dali's who was involved in Dali's estate contacted me. He loved our *Screams* and wanted to know if I'd like to license the Dali artwork and make inflatable clocks. To check it out, I had our Chinese factory make me a sample but it was too tacky, even for my taste. I then arranged for a latex clock sample to be made (it was way cool), showed it to my contact, who also liked it, and we agreed to make it happen.

Lesson Learned: Remember your niche and do market

research within your niche. I should have stuck with the inflatable clock. I forgot I make novelties, not hand-crafted art. Most people don't notice or care about the high degree of design we spent so much time on. Even the packaging – did anyone actually read all that stuff? Some market research would have been valuable. Maybe a tacky, inflatable clock would have been just the ticket.

Things got really complicated with our latex clock. Salvador Dalí died on January 23, 1989, having previously appointed the Spanish State as universal inheritor of all his goods, rights and artistic creations. It turned out that our Dali contact, also claiming ownership of some of the copyrights, was in a copyright dispute with the Spanish Government, by then represented by the Dali Foundation in Figuoro, Spain. And I had become a pawn.

The artist in me seized control from the businessperson in me. I would do anything to make our latex clock… in two versions! Why not? We had the money. Production turned out to be very complicated, even with the help of a specialized manufacturing company.

Lesson Learned: Bailing is not failing. I should have called it quits after investing in the special molds. I would have only been out $30,000.00, but I was on an Artistic Mission!

After traveling to France to meet with Dali's friend, I began dealings with the Dali Foundation; they assured me that they were the correct party to deal with. After long, complicated negotiations, we arrived at a contract. I paid an up front royalty guarantee, not unusual.

Lesson Learned: Avoid legal complications. Compromise – or bail out. You'd think that wrangling for copyright with the Spanish government and an international foundation would have killed the clocks. Instead, I continued my (insane) Artistic Mission!

To secure sales, I had approached my largest client, **The Museum Company** stores, with samples. Our buyer liked it and agreed to an order. They – and we – were doing really well with our *Scream* line and the notorious Van Gogh game, so we expected the clock to be a best seller, too. Remember the Golden Touch?

When the clocks arrived, the buyer refused them. It didn't matter why; the stores were just not going to carry them. If I had gotten the Museum Company to commit to a written purchase order, they would have been compelled to carry the clocks, but I hadn't. I had 15,000 clocks to sell. I was screwed.

Without the Museum Company, I had no easy way to penetrate my market on a mass scale. I would have to rely on individual art museum shops and our mom and pop stores. Even though the clocks were very cool, buyers balked at the price point. The large clocks were going to have to retail for $60.00, twice as much as anything we had sold before. We hadn't done market research on that new price point, and it was going to cost us! I lowered the price until I was selling them at nearly my cost. I was losing money, fast.

It was a nightmare. My whole business was now supporting the loss from clocks. I could only afford to pay the interest on my **line of credit**…$4,000.00 a month! Every single day for an entire year was awful. After another year, my bank sent two officers from the "troubled accounts division." When they walked into my office, they announced, "most people who we visit say this is the best day they've had in a long time." They were right.

The bankers helped me analyze my business and gave me a new loan where I would just be paying the principal…no interest! By this time they just wanted their money back. I busted my butt for the next two years paying off that loan and working to re-grow the business. I realized that I could no longer be the carefree artist running a company. I had a family and employees to support. I needed to make decisions about where I wanted not just my business to go but how I wanted to live my life. To make these decisions I needed a stable financial base, so regaining success became a driving force. I will also admit that I was afraid of what could happen if the bank called in the loan and I did not have the funds to pay it off: Bankruptcy? Lose my home? A destroyed reputation? And what would I do for work? I've only known how to be an artist, or an artist in business.

Butt-busting and accountability were critical, but what really saved us was our international reputation for unusual, high quality products and excellent customer service. This reputation attracted the attention of manufacturers looking to expand their markets.

$297,372.61

From the different manufacturers who approached me, I decided on two new product lines: **Magic Cubes** and **Thunder Tubes™**. They became the keys to a return to profitability. I was able to finally pay off my loan and I vowed to never borrow money for business again…I haven't.

Make sure you have a back up plan; I didn't. Even if we had had firm purchase orders, there was no guarantee that the clocks would have sold. If sales were poor, The Museum Company would not have reordered, and I would have been stuck with a lot of product anyway.

Take Action!

- ▶ Is Your *crazy idea* appropriately priced for your market, or is it over-designed? The consumer prefers simplicity. See what others are offering.

- ▶ Make sure you do financial planning. Work with someone who really knows how to evaluate and analyze your business and your books.

- ▶ If you get in over your head financially, what will you do?

- ▶ Do you have a diverse customer base? Make sure you do not rely on a single large client, or even a single client type. Changes in the financial marketplace or cultural shifts could rob you of a significant part of your income. How can you expand your customer type?

- ▶ Do you need to streamline your product line and maybe even your overall operation? Look to where you can cut costs.

- ▶ Decide if you have Inventory that needs to be sold on sale, at a deep discount, as a special offer or even liquidated. Sometimes it's better to just get rid of that bad decision even if you take a loss.

Might this be a time to sell your business? Have an honest conversation with yourself, your family and your advisors. It's your business – and your life.

29. Why are you Screaming?

 Fishtip™: Don't be too surprised when things suddenly change, they will.

Things are going perfectly!
- ☑ Your *crazy idea* is a hit.
- ☑ You're getting great publicity.
- ☑ Your employees all think like entrepreneurs.
- ☑ You just won a new car.
- ☑ Your kids were accepted into a great school on full scholarship.

Waiting for the hammer to drop?

No matter how good things get, from time to time your fortunes will likely slow, stall or race in reverse. But whatever befalls you, remember Hunter S. Thompson's famous words: *"When the going gets tough, the weird turn pro."*

Meaning: DON'T FREAK OUT!

What's happening to you has happened to someone else already. There are solutions to every problem, often simple ones, and there is always someone willing to help you.

As Lao Tzu said: *"Perseverance furthers."* I had hundreds of opportunities to say *"Enough, I quit!"* but I stuck with it. Affirmations, help from others, and your inner strength and will get you through the times when you want to give up.

Usually, people want to quit when things are the hardest. But the entrepreneur knows how to bend with adversity, how to surrender to unfavorable circumstances, how to stop resisting. By calming down and surrendering, you'll free up energy to find innovative solutions to your dilemma.

Remind yourself that you CAN do it. You had good reasons to begin this venture; just keep reminding yourself of those reasons the next time you want to quit!

Take Action!

▶ Look back at various problems you've had. How did you solve them? Were any truly unsolvable? What did you do as a result?

▶ Put something on the floor next to a long wall. Think of it like a game piece. Move it an inch a day. An inch isn't very much, but in a month it's clearly in a different place. Slow and steady will see you through.

▶ Bonus idea: Make a simple game out of the above Action Step and sell it, or give it to other new entrepreneurs.

Bumps in the Road

Over the years, I've encountered
plenty of bumps in the road.

You will, too.

Reviewing some of our bumps can
help you chart a smoother course.

Not bump-free – just smoother.

30. T/F ?: Nothing will go wrong.

 Fishtip™: Investigate disaster and inventory insurance.

 Fishtip™: Identify back-up sources for products and supplies.

 Fishtip™: Don't burn bridges with family, friends and business associates.

 Fishtip™: Get a reliable computer back up system and use it.

 Fishtip™: Always have a backup plan. (Sound familiar?)

Nothing will go wrong? Way false. Things will go wrong. It is hard to anticipate what we do not know. No matter how thoroughly you try to plan, something will be overlooked. Besides, in case you didn't already know this, not everything is in your control!

Every business has ups and downs, the idea being to have more of the ups. If you want to survive and continue to enjoy being an entrepreneur you must understand this and make contingency plans.

Some bumps in the road my company encountered:
- ordering from the factory too late for Q4 delivery
- ordering from the factory and forgetting that they were closed for holidays
- receiving defective goods because I didn't evaluate samples from each production run
- losing huge sales because I did not have a firm PO
- neglecting appropriate market research and ending up with a warehouse of overpriced goods
- loss of sales history on a computer crash (in prehistoric times, before routine backup systems)

If I had planned better and gotten more advice, I could have flattened many of these bumps, and cruised over the others more smoothly.

Your Day at the Office

Tipping your hat to Mad-Lib™, ask someone else to provide the fill-ins, then read out loud):

(First name #1) got a phone call from our (his/her) supplier. "We have a problem," said (foreign name). "There has been a (disaster) in (country) over the weekend and our (building type) where we keep all of our goods has been damaged."

"(Exclamation of dismay)," shouted (name #1). "What can we do?"

"Well," said (same foreign name), "There is another supplier in (another country), but they require being paid in (animal)."

"(Another exclamation of dismay)," said (First name #1).

"And that's not all," said (same foreign name). "If we don't confirm the order in (number from 1-10) hours, they'll sell the goods to our competition."

"(Exclamation of dismay #3)! What else could go wrong?"

"Actually," said (foreign name), the competition is your (family member), (new name to match gender of family member)."

"(Final exclamation of dismay)! (She / he) never forgave me from when I took (his/her) (noun) and never gave it back (number from 10-30) years ago!"

Take Action!

▶ Examine your production chain; brainstorm what can go wrong and have a back up plan in place.

▶ Examine and evaluate your office operations and brainstorm what can go wrong. Are there bottlenecks? Have a rescue plan in place.

▶ Build a reliable computer backup system.

DO IT NOW, TODAY, THIS INSTANT, NOW!

Back up everything, whether on-site or remote on the Internet. If you have paper records that are too cumbersome to scan, keep duplicates in a different, safe place. Include tax records, business receipts, employee records and hard copies of Invoices.

For computer back up, I use two drives. The current in-office drive backs up every night, the other is kept in a different location. I switch them on Mondays. With a terabyte drive costing around $150.00, there is NO REASON why you are not doing this. Even a flash drive can hold gigs of information.

Sing along: you know the words:
Always have a backup plan.

Selling The Scream

31. Is a giant order great news – or a bump?

 Fishtip™: Bigger is not always better. Consider carefully.

 Fishtip™: When considering a big order, make sure you can continue serving your other customers.

 Fishtip™: Maintain adequate inventory.

A friend of mine with an art reproduction company received a huge order for their posters, but had to prepay the UPS bill – over $10,000! The client paid late, but UPS wanted its money on time. She had to borrow money to pay UPS so UPS would keep shipping their goods to the rest of their clients. The interest on that loan came straight out of her profits. She, and I, learned that the "Wow!" of a big order can have as many pitfalls as benefits.

Now imagine that you have achieved success: orders are flowing in, just enough of just the right size so they are easily processed and you have a nice cash flow. Then one day you get your wish: a giant order. They want a LOT of your product, but here's the deal:

- You must follow their shipping instructions
- You must follow their payment guidelines
- You must meet their deadline, which may include fast turnaround on follow-up orders (Remember, get a firm PO!)

Potential pitfalls? Yup, always.

- Do you have the inventory to meet their first, and follow-up orders?
- Will there still be enough inventory to take care of your other established, and new customers?
- How will you decide if you should order extra inventory? How long will it take to receive it? Can you afford it? Will your personal banker give you a line of credit? Overseas manufacturers usually demand payment before they will ship the goods, and they rarely take credit cards. They want the money sent as a T/T, a bank wire transfer.

- If this big-order buyer wants discounted pricing, will it still be worthwhile to process their order? Will they reorder? (Success is in the reorders.)
- If you have to prepay shipping, will it affect your cash flow?
- Do you have the staffing to take care of everything?
- What are their payment terms? Will giving them **dating** hurt your cash flow, thus your own ability to not just pay your bills on time, but grow your business?
- Will taking care of them benefit you down the line: will they be loyal? Will they try new items? Will they continue to pay on time?

Big orders are usually good, but only if you plan for managing them and how it may affect your ability to service your current clients. While a big account can generate a lot of sales and thus profits, if they decide to stop ordering, you may loose a substantial part of your income. Maybe you even hired more employees or moved to a larger space based on the income from that one client; it happens all the time.

It is a balancing act; your smaller accounts may likely keep you in business. Also, they can be more personable to deal with. Those pleasant interactions will remind you of your initial entrepreneurial passion and why you got into this insanity in the first place.

Take Action!

▶ Have you ever had a giant order? Were you able to handle it? If you have not had a giant order, role play how you would handle it and identify potential problems. How will you solve them?

▶ Look at all areas of your business to see what problems a big demand could have. Plan for those problems.

▶ Make sure your smaller clients are happy and feeling well served. Send out a thank you mailing such as a card with a handwritten note, not an email, and include a special offer. Your clients will recognize that you really care about them.

Selling The Scream

32. Bump: Sure we can make that for you.

 Fishtip™: Create unique products and establish intellectual property protection.

 Fishtip™: Especially with ideas and new products, be careful what you say – and what others say to you.

 Fishtip™: With legal documents, read the whole thing and ask questions. Don't sign until you understand every word; later is probably too late.

 Fishtip™: Make sure all contract signers are authorized to sign.

 Fishtip™: Business is business; don't take it personally.

Here's the story of one of the biggest bumps for our company so far. We decided to make a *Scream* mousepad. Our *Scream* line was doing well over all, and our largest client wanted to carry the mousepads in their 50+ stores. I found a mousepad manufacturer, even Made in the USA! They produced quality goods, and their pricing would work.

The samples they provided looked great, and we ordered 10,000 pieces. We had another company custom make nice window boxes, and we assembled everything in our warehouse.

The mousepads sold fast. Ten months later we ordered another 10,000 pieces and then eight months later another 5,000. Then I discovered that our manufacturer was making their own *"The Scream"* mousepad, in direct competition with us. I was stunned – and really, really pissed off. They never asked if it was OK. They never asked if they could license our design or work with us in any other way.

But then, why should they? I didn't have a **non-compete**

agreement with them. Such documents usually have a certain term, like 3-5 years, during which they cannot make or sell similar products. It just never crossed my mind; in fact, I had never heard of a non-compete agreement. It wasn't like they were overseas, slipping product out the back door. They were right here in America, knocking off our idea.

Legally there was not a lot we could do as *"The Scream"* painting was in the public domain in the US and they legally had the right to make a similar product (unlike our inflatables, keychains and t-shirts which had our own copyrighted artwork). But ethically, *How Could They???*

So, I did what I could: I called the president of the manufacturing company. I don't remember my exact words, but I do remember his. When I said something like, "You mean you would rather make money from your version then have us as happy and loyal customers?" He replied, "Yes."

I was furious, but what could I do? Because of their own extensive market penetration, and because they controlled the means of production, they controlled the cost of our mousepad. Additionally, they had a lot of their own mousepad designs, and serviced many of the same clients. So after selling the last 5,000 pieces we just dropped the mousepad from our line.

Could we have found another manufacturer? Could we have sold more, even with their direct competition? Probably, but not without a struggle, so we just moved on. In this case, I knew when to bail.

OK, I'll admit it. I really wanted to kill that guy. Of course, I wouldn't, really, but that was my initial reaction. OK, so what could I do about my frustration:

- Stick pins in a voodoo doll?
- Whack a punching bag?
- Spend an hour at an indoor shooting range?
- Play my drums?
- Chop wood?
- Do yard work?
- Tai chi?

- Meditate?
- Just breathe?
- Just fuggeddabowdit?

And what could I do about them?
- Report them to their local Better Business Bureau?
- Write a letter to the editor of their local newspaper?
- Let other people in my field know what happened with a warning to avoid them?

Taking a cue from my product line, *I Screamed Real Loud*. Then I chopped wood, did yard work and breathed. I wrote a business association in their area, and I warned other vendors to avoid them.

Lesson learned: My intense reaction was both due to how this would hurt my business, and how I took it personally. That was the artist in me: I felt insulted, like they were stepping all over my paintings or stealing my music! The fact is, from their point of view, they just made a smart business decision.

> *"Your best teacher is your last mistake."*
>
> Ralph Nader

Success breeds copies and copiers. Everyone in business is looking for opportunities. Some people will ask to license a property, while others may just "borrow." It happens at trade shows all the time: with cell phone cameras you can be sure your new, *crazy idea* is being "documented."

Take Action ...when developing a new product!

All of this may sound scary, or that you can't trust anyone, or that people will think you are paranoid, but honest business folks will respect you for your careful planning; it protects them, too.

- ▶ Check and make sure your idea is truly original, that you are not violating someone else's protected work.
- ▶ If there is a way to secure Intellectual Property Protection,

Bump: Sure we can make that for you. 141

do it, via a copyright, patent or trademark.

- ▶ Don't give out information until you do have protection. Speak in generalities.
- ▶ Get non-compete and **non-disclosure agreements** with your manufacturers, sales reps, and employees.
- ▶ Be careful about letting other people tell you about their ideas It may be similar to something you are already working on, or that you might want to work on someday. They can then claim you stole the idea from them. Sounds extreme but it happens.
- ▶ If you connect up with an inventor's group or an idea website, make really sure you understand what you are exposing yourself to. Once you announce an idea, it may enter the public domain.

"It is a waste of time to be angry about my disability. One has to get on with life and I haven't done badly. People won't have time for you if you are always angry or complaining."

Stephen Hawking
Physicist

"My mother used to say, "He who angers you, conquers you!" But my mother was a saint."

Elizabeth Kenny
Australian pioneering physical therapist

"When angry, count to four, when very angry, swear."

Mark Twain
Author and humorist

33. Legal Schmeegal

BLAH BLAH BLAH BLAH BLAH BLAH BLAH BLAH BLAH BLAH
BLAH BLAH BLAH BLAH BLAH BLAH BLAH BLAH BLAH BLAH
BLAH BLAH BLAH BLAH BLAH BLAH BLAH OFFER LAH BLAH
BLAH BLAH BLAH BLAH BLAH BLAH BLAH BLAH BLAH BLAH
BLAH BLAH BLAH BLAH BLAH BLAH BLAH BLAH BLAH BLAH
BLAH BLAH BLAH BLAH BLAH BLAH BLAH BLAH BLAH BLAH
BLAH BLAH BLAH BLAH BLAH BLAH BLAH BLAH BLAH BLAH
BLAH BLAH BLAH BLAH BLAH BLAH BLAH BLAH BLAH BLAH
BLAH BLAH BLAH BLAH BLAH BLAH BLAH BLAH BLAH BLAH
BLAH BLAH BLAH BLAH BLAH BLAH BLAH BLAH BLAH BLAH
BLAH BLAH BLAH BLAH BLAH BLAH BLAH BLAH BLAH BLAH
BLAH BLAH BLAH BLAH BLAH BLAH BLAH BLAH BLAH BLAH
BLAH BLAH BLAH BLAH BLAH BLAH BLAH BLAH BLAH BLAH
BLAH BLAH BLAH BLAH BLAH BLAH BLAH BLAH BLAH BLAH
BLAH BLAH BLAH BLAH BLAH BLAH BLAH BLAH BLAH BLAH
BLAH BLAH BLAH BLAH BLAH BLAH BLAH BLAH BLAH BLAH
BLAH BLAH BLAH BLAH BLAH BLAH BLAH BLAH BLAH BLAH
BLAH BLAH ACCEPTANCE AH BLAH BLAH BLAH BLAH BLAH
BLAH BLAH BLAH BLAH BLAH BLAH BLAH BLAH BLAH BLAH
BLAH BLAH BLAH BLAH BLAH BLAH BLAH BLAH BLAH BLAH
BLAH BLAH BLAH BLAH BLAH BLAH BLAH BLAH BLAH BLAH
BLAH BLAH BLAH BLAH BLAH BLAH BLAH BLAH BLAH BLAH
BLAH BLAH BLAH BLAH BLAH BLAH BLAH BLAH BLAH BLAH
BLAH BLAH BLAH BLAH BLAH BLAH BLAH BLAH BLAH BLAH
BLAH BLAH BLAH BLAH BLAH BLAH BLAH BLAH BLAH BLAH
BLAH BLAH BLAH BLAH BLAH BLAH BLAH BLAH BLAH BLAH
BLAH BLAH BLAH BLAH BLAH BLAH BLAH BLAH BLAH BLAH
BLAH BLAH BLAH BLAH CONSIDERATION BLAH BLAH BLAH
BLAH BLAH BLAH BLAH BLAH BLAH BLAH BLAH BLAH BLAH
BLAH BLAH BLAH BLAH BLAH BLAH BLAH BLAH BLAH BLAH
BLAH BLAH BLAH BLAH BLAH BLAH BLAH BLAH BLAH BLAH
BLAH BLAH BLAH BLAH BLAH BLAH BLAH BLAH BLAH BLAH
BLAH BLAH BLAH BLAH BLAH BLAH BLAH BLAH BLAH BLAH
BLAH BLAH BLAH BLAH BLAH BLAH BLAH BLAH BLAH BLAH

OFFER ACCEPTANCE CONSIDERATION

Did you find these three words hidden in the "contract" on the previous page? These are the guts of every contract and service agreement. With legal documents, read everything and ask questions. Don't sign until you understand every word; later is probably too late.

These endless documents use cumbersome language. Our eyes glaze over. We get drowsy, careless and impatient when we try to comprehend these foreign sounding things. Once you sign, though, you are bound by every word.

I'll admit, I have clicked "OK" many, many times when accepting a software license without reading the whole thing. So have you. But what if some joker inserted "plus you must come to my home on Sundays and do my laundry. Then fold everything and put in the correct drawer. If you fail to abide by this license and its stipulations then you and your successors hereby assign all your assets including but not limited to…"

OK, this goofy example may not hold up long in court, but we are agreeing to abide by whatever we sign.

The basics of a contract are three things: Here's my own *crazy Idea* as an example:

Offer: I (my company) propose to license the image of *"The Scream"* to use on products to sell worldwide under certain terms and conditions.

Acceptance: The Munch Museum agrees to grant the license, making me (my company) legally bound by my offer.

Consideration: (something of value I include with my offer) I (my company) will make an up-front payment of $X,000.00 to be applied against a royalty rate of Y% on all sales of the products as described herein for the term as stipulated.

Consideration can also be stated more generally, such as the following: *In consideration of the mutual promises and undertakings herein contained, and for other good and valuable consideration, the receipt and sufficiency of which are hereby acknowledged, the parties hereby agree as follows:* then all the rest of the important blah blah blah....

Of course there may be many details to include. Make sure all of your concerns are addressed when negotiating a deal. Contracts basically state who is responsible for what by when, who gets what, what will happen if you don't do your end of the deal and how conflicts are to be arbitrated. Sounds pretty straight forward, but society has gone so litigation crazy that what used to be a firm handshake while looking in someone's eyes has grown to seemingly endless pages of blah blah blah. A contract I had with the Andy Warhol Foundation for the Visual Arts was 42 pages long, and it was just for one of our little Magic Cubes. I read the whole thing and made sure I understood every paragraph and clause and addendum before I signed it. I even suggested and was able to make some changes; that won't happen if you do not read it.

Read anything you are signing your name to. Insist everyone else reads it as well and that all signers have the power and authority to sign. If someone is put off by a contract, determine their specific concerns. Maybe the concern can be worked out. Remember that it is a negotiation. If both parties have a genuine interest in reaching an agreement, both will offer concessions. You have to decide what is important to you for your business and what you are willing to give up on, and how much. If you can't work it out, maybe the time is not right to do business together. Maybe come back at a later date and make your offer again. Maybe work through a third party that knows you both.

A contract protects all parties; it doesn't mean that you don't trust someone, or that they don't trust you. A contract is just a way to make sure that work was performed as originally agreed to. Like a business plan, it is a way to measure and gauge progress. If things work out, it becomes a blueprint that can be extended and expanded.

(See Resources for two web sites offering free legal forms. Google "free contract forms" for others. Most Agreements though are so specific you will want to work with a lawyer.)

Take Action!

▶ If you have signed any contracts, read and reread the whole thing. Are you happy with everything you signed your name to?

▶ Read one of those long software agreements or social networking agreements. What the heck do they say?

▶ Read a privacy information contract, then decide if you want to opt out of sharing your information.

▶ As an exercise, make the simplest contract you can to sell someone a tennis ball. Remember: offer, acceptance, consideration. Try to think of everything that is important to cover to protect yourself. Then take a look at terms of selling and buying on eBay. Then look back at your tennis ball contract. Are you still protected?

"Put any lawyer joke here."

From The Screameria:

10/15/1996, from T.L Hannah High School in Anderson, NC:

Dear Sirs: Enclosed is a photograph for the *Scream* Museum that was taken in my office adjacent to the art room. We have been collecting *Scream* items for several years: cards, jokes, books, posters, T-shirts, ties, etc. Your large *Scream* stands in one corner of the room. My students and I think that your dolls are fun. Please let me know if you have any other *Scream* items. We are always excited with a new 'find' to add to the collection.

◉ ◉ ◉

(On the rare occasion that someone received a defective *Scream*, we asked them to cut off the head and mail it back as proof of purchase.)

4/17/1995: I am sending you this head in good faith. A few friends came to my house and we had a few farewell drinks. A poem was written:

You blessed us with your presence only for a time
When I first blew you up I thought that you were fine
But as each day went by you seemed to wilt and fold
That air that brings you life your body would not hold.
I tried to save you, as if I were a medic
The glue I was using started giving me a headache.
I had to finally admit that you were losing the fight
Why you? Why me? This doesn't seem Right!
When I put you out of your misery, it seemed as
*   if a dream,*
A dreaded day it was when "I" killed the Scream.

Selling The Scream

34. Bump: You don't want to sell my stuff anymore?

 Fishtip™: Continually find new sales opportunities.

Lots of stores were doing well selling our *Scream* products: something striking to bring people into the store, good profit margin, repeat orders. Then, after a number of years, some stores decided they didn't want to carry *Scream* stuff any more.

"What? You don't want to sell our *Screams* any more?"
"No, we think it's about time to stop."
"Why?" I asked, almost in a panic, "Aren't they selling?"
"Yeah, they still sell, but we just think it's time for a change."

They're going to stop selling our great-selling product because "it's time for a change?" WTF? How dare they?

Reality check: it's likely not personal, it's business*. There can be so many reasons why a store stops carrying a product or even an entire line. Maybe they just want a different look in their store. Maybe they want the space for something with a smaller **footprint** or higher profit margin. Maybe staff doesn't want to look at inflatables screaming in anguish any more. Maybe a customer said the *Screams* were downers. Maybe the store got some defective product.

> *Then again, maybe it is personal!* Maybe the store had a bad experience with your sales rep or delivery driver or – could it be? – *you*.

What can you do? Be a problem-solver. Ask the store's specific reasons, and be understanding of their situation. Maybe you can keep your product in that store after all. If not, what you learn can only help as you serve other clients. See this as an opportunity to explore possible new products, or new clients, or even a new client category. Could your product be educational?

Could your product be a give-away **premium or promotional item**? Could it be an added-value addition to someone else's product or service? We sold *Scream* inflatables to a financial services company that used them to comically calm down their clients during a market crisis. Be proactive.

Offer your retreating client a better deal. If you have other products, see if the store wants to sell them. For sure, ask if you can contact the store in a year to see if they want to pick it up again. Ask them for suggestions on what you could make; maybe they already have something percolating in their mind that they'd love to see. You could even suggest someone else's product line. If you do, that client will remember you as The Problem Solver, and eventually, it will come back to you in a positive way.

Just don't burn your bridges. Word spreads fast and you want to "all ways and always" maintain a good reputation. If a client is no fun to deal with, or difficult, or even awful, just say your most pleasant "Thanks" and don't do business with them again. Other potential clients are just waiting for you to help them grow their own businesses. Be their solution.

Take Action!

▶ Reintroduce your products to old clients that don't use them anymore. How can you make your stuff seem fresh again?

▶ Ask your clients for suggestions on who you could approach for sales.

▶ Invite some creative people over for lunch. Explain ahead of time that you want everybody to brainstorm crazy ways you could position your *crazy idea* so that it will be attractive to new client types. Offer the participants an honorarium for their help.

> *"We are always saying to ourself...we have to innovate. We've got to come up with breakthroughs. In fact, the way software works.. so long as you are using your existing software.. you don't pay us anything at all. So we're only paid for breakthroughs."*

Bill Gates
Founder of Microsoft

> *"...now that I'm selling spaghetti sauce (with Newman's Own), I begin to understand the romance of business.. the allure of being the biggest fish in the pond and the juice you get from beating out your competitors."*

Paul Newman
Actor and entrepreneur

35. Cubes and Tubes to the Rescue

 Fishtip™: When you are feeling desperate, step back, get quiet and listen. Opportunities are everywhere but you won't recognize them if your mind is full of shouting.

 Fishtip™: Remember the Power of Yes! Yes you CAN do it!

 Fishtip™: When facing uncertainty, don't assume you have to fix what is broken; you may need to find a different direction to achieve success.

> *"Without the strength to endure the crisis, one will not see the opportunity within. It is within the process of endurance that opportunity reveals itself."*
>
> Chin-Ning Chu
> *Author and Speaker, she is known as The Master Strategist, basing her teachings on Sun Tzu's Art of War*

If it wasn't for our excellent reputation for product design and customer service, and my dogged perseverance, the Dali Clock goof would have wiped out my company. Fortunately, our successes attracted the attention of other companies wishing to enter the gift marketplace. Plus, I was exactly ready for something new. Magic Cubes and Thunder Tubes™ were the keys to climbing out of the Dali Clock pit and becoming profitable once again.

Magic Cubes
For three years in a row I exhibited our products at Museum Expressions, a museum trade show held in Paris at the Louvre. We made quite a splash the first year as our inflatables won the

Coup de Coeur (translates roughly as "Really Cool" or "Dude!").
A company also exhibiting approached us with a product I had
never seen before, the Magic Cube. Sold mostly as a premium or
tourist souvenir, it is a small cube that at first looks like a version
of the Rubik's Cube; but it is not. A Magic Cube is made of eight
smaller cubes hinged in a clever way that allows it to be continuously opened and folded, revealing 3-6 surprise images on the
inside, in addition to the six on the outside. The manufacturer, who
had heard of our success with selling the *Scream* was looking for
companies to begin selling cubes as museum gift items, and offered us exclusive US distributorship for the museum market. I was
immediately captivated by the gizmo's possibilities, and accepted
on the spot.

We started out with two themes meant to appeal to a general audience: "Art Masterpieces from the Renaissance and Impression-
ism," and "Egypt." The themes quickly became so popular that we
grew the line to over 50 titles, with 40 additional custom designs for
clients' promotional programs. In five years we sold over 500,000
pieces; I then sold this line to another company. That gave me the financial freedom to pursue other interests, including writing this book!

Thunder Tubes™
I am a musician and make some of my own instruments, occasionally for sale. Several years into *Scream* production, I was exhibiting
a line of custom designed, giant twirl drums I developed for the
Percussive Arts Society's annual conference. Remo Belli, President
of Remo, Inc, came by my booth, looked up at my ten foot tall,
monster twirl drum and remarked "…never seen that before."

Monster comment! This was *the* Remo of world-renowned Remo,
Inc. This company was both an early developer of synthetic drum
heads and also revolutionized global music-making by making
world-music drums available to the public. Thousands and thousands of professional and amateur musicians in almost every
country use Remo percussion for everything from professional
performances to casual drum circles.

Later that day, Remo suggested I visit their factory in LA to see
a project they were working on. When I showed up a couple of
months later, he showed me their newest product, the Spring

Drum. It's basically a small, one-headed drum with a spring hanging down from the center of the drumhead. Shaking the instrument allows the drumhead to greatly amplify the spring vibrations and produces a sound akin to thunder, lions roaring, UFOs landing.... Playing with the spring and covering and uncovering the open end produces an even wider assortment of sounds. It has such amazing capabilities yet is so simple. I thought they were magic the first time I encountered them, and still do.

Remo was fascinated by the market I served: museum shops and general, novelty gift stores. Did I think I could sell the Spring Drum to my customers? Oh YEAH! We cut a deal.

Spring Drums were so cool; my mind worked overtime. I changed (and trademarked) the name to the Thunder Tube™ (more compelling and memorable), and added striking graphics and new packaging. The drums themselves needed some modifications to lower the price point. I also included basic instructions for how to make a variety of sounds.

Thunder Tubes™ were instant hits with the general toy market, plus many new markets: storytellers, science teachers, theaters, film/video/audio producers, therapists who work with autistic children... even people who help desensitize animals to loud sounds. I also greatly expanded the sales to and use of Thunder Tubes™ by musicians.

Thunder Tubes™ continue to generate revenues for my company, for Remo, Inc., and for Trophy Music in Cleveland, Ohio. Trophy markets and distributes the line and fulfills orders, Remo remains the manufacturer and pays us a licensing fee to also sell Thunder Tubes™, which they recognize as my trademarked item.

Trophy also handles my other two music products: the Washboard Tie™ (see next chapter) and our mini Skull Shakers, our unique answer to generic egg shakers. Egg shakers are just that: egg-shaped and -sized mini-maracas, filled with tiny beads. They are percussion instruments and are sold in every music store. They are also easy to print on, so are frequently given away as promotional items. Remembering my formula of Weird = Great, *crazy Idea*, we introduced our Skull Shakers, which have proven to be steady sellers.

Our relationships with Remo and Trophy are wonderful examples of how to create and manage **multiple revenue streams**.

Take Action!

▶ Look around and see what other opportunities there may be to re-start your company

▶ Do you see someone else's product that suffers from under-performance? Can you reinvent it and come to an agreement where you will mutually benefit from its rebirth?

"Chance is always powerful. Let your hook be always cast. In the pool where you least expect it there will be fish."

Ovid
Ancient Roman poet who wrote about love, seduction, and mythological transformation

"The harder you work, the luckier you get."

Gary Player
Professional Golfer

Power Demo:
Selling Tubes and Ties in Person

When I do trade shows and performances, people invariably ask how to make sounds with the Thunder Tube™.

I could just point out the printed instructions included in every package, but wouldn't a more dynamic approach generate more interest and be more fun for everybody? So I created a performance called "I Am a Mad Inventor." Kids and grown-ups love it. Speaking and singing only in rhymes, I go through basic and advanced ways to produce Thunder Tube™ sounds. I evolved the concept to also demonstrate how to use not just the Thunder Tube™, but any instrument, in new ways.

The performance increases the Tubes' mystique: "Tubes are cool. Cool people have Tubes. I'll be cool and do cool stuff with it if I have one." Product placement in TV and movies is a little like this, though more subtle.

I created another performance piece with our Washboard Tie™, invented by my friend Laura Geisen. I vocalize music from all over the world while putting the tie through its paces. These "demo entertainments" are flexible: they can last 40 minutes for 400 kids in a school gym, be part of a formal concert in a theater, or be a one minute blast for a crush of curious customers pausing at your trade show booth. Once potential customers are paying attention, I give a group lesson. There is nothing like having them hold the real deal in their hands and make their own magic to close a sale.

Selling The Scream

36. Remaking a Product

 Fishtip™: Explore ways to expand business on the *crazy ideas* you already sell.

 Fishtip™: Before you hire outside experts, encourage your own staff to brainstorm.

It is not always necessary to invent a new product to increase revenue.

With Magic Cubes, we repositioned an existing product for a different market, from a promotional give-away to a classy museum gift. We also upgraded the packaging: each cube comes in a full-color box and has a detailed, fold-out pamphlet describing the cube's theme plus the specifics of each image.

With Thunder Tubes™ we gave an existing product a new image, and expanded its customer base beyond just musicians to include many new users.

We also became the world-wide distributor for the clip-on Zydeco Tie™, invented by my friend Laura Geisen. Laura was at a Zydeco concert, enjoying the music and envying the musicians on stage. She watched the washboard player, wishing she could join in. "I wish there was something I could just hang around my neck and play, like…a tie!" That was her AHA! moment.

A Zydeco Tie™ is basically a steel necktie, ribbed like a washboard, that you play with thimbles. Like the Thunder Tube™, it is jaw-dropping cool and draws a crowd with the first sounds it makes. Like with Thunder Tubes™, we gave the Zydeco Tie™ a make-over. We renamed it the Washboard Tie™ and gave it new packaging, since washboards are more familiar to people than Zydeco music. We then offered it to our already huge group of Thunder Tube™ clients and the increase in sales confirmed our decision to carry this new product.

In each case, with the Thunder Tube™, Magic Cube and Washboard Tie™, we took an existing product, invented by someone else, and created such compelling new identities that not only did sales increase a LOT, but everyone thinks I invented them. Though I am quick to credit the actual inventor, that assumption about my relationship to these products is a mark of my marketing success. I will admit that I do sometimes pass myself off as the Galactic Ambassador of the Tubes and Ties, to which kids reply, "Really?"

You can also create new products by licensing; you use someone else's existing imagery or products in the development of your new idea. It's very common. For instance, most products you see based on Disney, Marvel or Star Wars characters are made by another company that has paid for the rights to make the products. In general, a licensing contract allows you to make very specific products in certain quantities and sell them to certain areas in the world (territories) for a specified length of time.

Example: our license with the Smithsonian Institute for our George Caitlin Indian Gallery Magic Cube allowed us to make 3,000 pieces and sell them worldwide for two years. If we did well and wanted to make a reprint, or wanted to extend the time period, we would need to re-negotiate with the Smithsonian.

We've established licensing agreements with dozens of organizations, including:
- Munch Museum, Norway
- Chicago Art institute
- Smithsonian Institution
- Metropolitan Museum of Art, New York
- Salvador Dali Museum, St. Petersburg, FL
- American Folk Art Museum, New York
- Asian Art Museum, San Francisco
- American Folk Art Museum
- Asia Society New York
- Salvador Dali Foundation, Spain
- Andy Warhol Foundation for the Visual Arts
- Albert Einstein Estate

Licensing your properties to others is another way to create a revenue stream. Just as we license our Thunder Tube™ to Remo, you may be able to license your designs, products, software applications, industrial processes, or even trademarked names.

160　　　*Selling The Scream*

The point is, there are many ways to breathe new life into an existing product by modifying it, changing its name, repackaging it, finding new uses for it or introducing it to new audiences.

Just look around. First, look at your own products; maybe the key to your company's next success is right in front of you. Then, ask your staff for ideas. Does someone have a *crazy idea* they've been waiting to share? Make sure your company encourages and rewards innovation.

Some Places to Find Inspiration

Visit museums, trade shows, and all kinds of stores. Go to a big bookstore and look at all the magazines. Go to the library or online and get membership magazines for niche markets. Look at catalogs: people sell everything, and some of it needs improvement! Flip through Skymall Magazine next time you fly; it's chock full of mostly unnecessary but ingenious devices. Check this book's **Resources** for beginning points to surf the web. There are oceans of ideas floating around the Internet.

Take Action!

▶ Think of how you can add to the mythology of your *crazy idea* by creating stories, songs, ads, and events. Put up You Tube videos and make them fun. Give your product to others who can use it in new ways. Their creativity is a fabulous form of marketing. For example, salesmen like to begin meetings with the Washboard Tie™. They start talking, play a few notes, and blow everyone's mind.

▶ Go to a grocery store and practice renaming products; be smart, be ridiculous, be irreverent, have fun. The key to a product's success is its name, followed by its attributes, then its price. Names that are easy to say or that rhyme always do better.

▶ Have a meeting with your staff. Brainstorm new ideas. First look at your current offerings, then go for totally new ideas. Don't worry about practicality; just get the juices flowing. No staff? Invite over trusted, creative friends for two hours of their time; then give them a great lunch.

- What would you like to license from someone else? What would you do with it? What is keeping you from pursuing this idea?

- Do you have anything that might be valuable to another company? Maybe they can be successful where you could not…. Collect royalties.

> "What has been will be again, what has been done will be done again; there is nothing new under the sun."
>
> Ecclesiastes 1:9-14

My friend Diane Katzman started a retail jewelry business. She was doing okay but needed to expand in some other direction for her company to grow. She began offering her line as corporate gifts. This actually led to custom pieces created for specific companies who both gave them out as thank you's to their customers and used them in-house to celebrate milestones. She then began donating them to her local National Public Radio station affiliate who gave them away to listeners renewing their memberships. While she didn't make any money from these donations, her name and company name were mentioned constantly during the 3-10 days of the fund drive…this became an essential part of her marketing plan which the radio station is all too happy to partner with. This on-air exposure often provided her with new clients.

37. You spent an hour doing what?

 Fishtip™: Make lists and follow them. Think of them as short-term business plans.

 Fishtip™: Build ways for your staff to help you stay on task.

As a "creative-type" and an artist (How many times have I used that excuse?), as someone whose life revolves around the question, "What would happen if… ?" I'm not always the greatest at staying on task. My kindergarten teacher put a curse on me: I still have the note she wrote to my first grade teacher, "Robert should do well next year, he is curious about everything." I am.

"What would happen if?" Unfortunately, I only applied this principal to my art making, not my business. In hindsight, it would have been a smart way to run out a scenario like, "What would happen if the Museum Company didn't want to sell our Dali Clocks?" Just like you brainstorm for ideas, you should, as I mentioned earlier, take time to brainstorm for disaster and success.

Eventually though, I taught myself to make lists. Of course, you have to know where the list is and actually do the stuff on it, maybe even in an order such as "most important first." What novel ideas.

I'm still easily distracted, though, and get sidetracked, wander from thing to thing, or spend time on unnecessary tasks. For instance, in replying to a French client, I spent an hour composing the email in French. It was challenging and fun and I learned a few new phrases. But the client was a fluent English-reader; I could have typed the email in five minutes. Fun? Uh huh. Waste of time? Yup!

Keeping your company "on task" is a good reason for creative types to get business partners. The artist can generate new ideas while the business person keeps the business ship afloat, and sailing more efficiently and further.

Take Action!

▶ Make a daily and weekly to-do list. Are the most important tasks at the beginning or the end of the list? Sometimes we put the fun or easiest stuff on top even though it is not really that important to get done right away.

▶ No staff? Have the meeting with yourself. Talk out loud if necessary…it helps.

▶ Mark LeBlanc, author of *Growing Your Business*, suggests completing three high value activities every day. Even if they are simple, by the end of a month you will have accomplished 90 things…that is a LOT!

▶ Begin each day with a meeting: To Do.

▶ End each day with a meeting: What got done.

38. Are you running an innovative business or just running?

 Fishtip™: To stay inspired and successful, periodically step back, reformulate your plan, and get help.

You had your great *crazy idea*. You made a plan that you are following. Things are moving along….and they are also getting more complex. Customer Service takes more time as you sell more products and get more accounts. You have to pay much closer attention to cash flow. The timing of manufacturing, factory shipping and customer delivery is getting trickier. And you're still doing so many things yourself…Oy!

Pull back, maybe go on a retreat, and figure out how to proceed. If you don't have a business advisor yet, do it now!

Are you enabling your employees to reach their full potentials – and make maximum contributions to your company? Trust them and give them more responsibility. The more responsibility you hand off, the more time you'll have to focus on the fun stuff that got you into this in the first place - *crazy ideas*.

I had to do everything myself at first, but even after I hired employees, I micro-managed and didn't effectively encourage and enable my employees to help grow the business. Looking back, I can see that they tried to do more, to offer more, but I never surrendered enough control. The result was slow growth, and occasional stagnation.

Even if you have only a few employees, trust and encourage them and enable them to stretch themselves professionally. If, after getting their assigned tasks completed they can also help your company grow, acknowledge that wonderful benefit. But why should employees care if they help your company – unless they get rewarded for doing so? Really. It could be money or praise or satisfaction or sense of achievement or concrete proof of achievement or acknowledgement inside/outside the company or a better job title or a promotion….If you want your employees to contribute to your company's success, they need to know how they will share in that success.

Dealing with employees can be one of the toughest things about growing a business. Many of us are so used to doing things by ourselves that we get lost in the details and forget that we are trying to reach a big goal. Let go of micromanaging, or you'll handle day-to-day details, but miss the big stuff – including the big opportunities that appear.

As a new entrepreneur, you started with an innovative vision: you were on fire! Your contagious enthusiasm inspired others and they wanted to help you succeed. If you get caught in the details, your fire will dim. You, and those around you, will be less inspired, and sales will flatten. You'll run the risk of business failure, which is much more common that success. Keep your fire burning!

Take Action!

- ▶ Imagine what your ideal company would be like, especially what kind of people would be working there. Now go find them!

- ▶ What can you offer to employees who contribute to your company's success?

- ▶ Talk to the owners of other small companies and ask them the following questions in confidence:
  - How has it been dealing with employees?
  - Did you have a hard time giving up control?
  - Would you structure your workforce the same if you could do it over?
  - What do you suggest as a way to attract the best employees?
  - Have you ever had to fire an employee? How did it go?

"We want passion for our business...workers who can interpret and execute our mission, who want to build a career, not just take a temporary job."

Howard Schultz
Founder of Starbucks

> *"Research indicates that workers have three prime needs: Interesting work, recognition for doing a good job, and being let in on things that are going on in the company."*

Zig Ziglar
American author, salesperson, and motivational speaker

> *"The people who are doing the work are the moving force behind the Macintosh. My job is to create a space for them, to clear out the rest of the organization and keep it at bay."*

Steve Jobs
Co-founder, Chairman, and CEO of Apple Inc.

From The Screameria:

A woman called from New York City. She'd been on Wall Street, delivering an inflated *Scream* to a friend who had just lost her job. When she opened the taxi door, a gust of wind sucked the *Scream* right out of the taxi and into the air…gone!

☻　☻　☻

Later that day another New Yorker called: "Hello, I live on the 27th floor of a high rise near Lincoln Center. You're not going to believe this, but one of your inflatable *Screams* just flew right by my picture window!"

39. Corporate Entrepreneurship = Intrapreneurship

As an entrepreneur, you not only want to have a vision for your company to follow, you want to create an environment where everyone in the organization will be valued for their contributions, especially beyond their job description.

I recently spoke to a class of MBA students. They all held jobs at a variety of successful companies, and wanted to know how to foster a greater sense of entrepreneurship amongst all employees, companywide. Sometimes this is referred to as intrapreneurship –entrepreneurship within a bigger company.

The lessons I've learned apply to any intrapreneurial project, whether service-based or for-profit, whether neighborhood or global – any businesses wanting employees to find innovative solutions to company growth and efficiency. Any company that is not continually adapting to the evolving business environment and to new technologies may be making an unintentional decision to go out of business. You've heard it before: innovate or die.

Most important, company leaders must encourage risk taking. Like a school principal, top management establishes workplace climate. If everyone is only allowed to do the status quo, if mistakes are punished, and if managers are seen as egotistic authorities, this company will not be an enjoyable place to work, nor will it be an industry leader. If management encourages risk-taking, celebrates successes and encourages learning from mistakes, the company can keep moving forward.

Taking that first step can be scary because it means breaking thought-patterns and routines and introducing new ways of doing things. The familiar is replaced by the unknown.

Given the right climate though, employees will step up with suggestions on everything from how to improve operations and customer service to ideas for new products. A factory sees a way to modify an industrial process and reduce accidents or save thousands, even millions, in time and materials. An office worker finds a faster, cheaper supply source. Another identifies software that will streamline record keeping. Someone suggests a new market or a new product…. Think of it as a suggestion box, but it is no longer necessary to be anonymous.

The following products and services were all developed by motivated individuals who saw opportunities within large companies that support innovation. Though all of these *crazy ideas* became very successful, the developers often had to convince many other people in the company that it was a worthwhile pursuit: that it could actually be done, that it could be expanded to work within the entire organization and that it could generate a profit (see Resources to learn more about each of these intrapreneurial innovations).

- Post-it Notes
- Glide Floss
- Sony Play Station
- Java Programming Language
- Digital Light Processing Technology (Video Projectors)
- ELIXIR Guitar Strings
- Looj Gutter Cleaning Robot
- Caribou Coffee Customer Loyalty Program

Take Action

- ▶ What are you going to transform in your company?
- ▶ What difference will it make?
- ▶ Who do you need to speak to, to make it happen?
- ▶ What resources do you need?
- ▶ How will you know it's worked?

> *"Most new jobs won't come from our biggest employers. They will come from our smallest. We've got to do everything we can to make entrepreneurial dreams a reality."*
>
> Ross Perot
> Businessman

"Nobody talks of entrepreneurship as survival, but that's exactly what it is and what nurtures creative thinking."

Anita Roddick
Founder of The Body Shop
chain of cosmetic stores

"Anyone who has never made a mistake has never tried anything new."

Albert Einstein
Physicist and Pacifist

"When you innovate, you've got to be prepared for everyone telling you you're nuts."

Larry Elison
Co-founder of Oracle Corporation

The Future

It's now.

"The Internet will help achieve "friction free capitalism" by putting buyer and seller in direct contact and providing more information to both about each other."

Bill Gates
Founder of Microsoft

"I must confess that I've never trusted the Web. I've always seen it as a coward's tool. Where does it live? How do you hold it personally responsible? Can you put a distributed network of fiber-optic cable "on notice"? And is it male or female? In other words, can I challenge it to a fight?"

Stephen Colbert
Comedian, satirist, actor and writer and host of The Colbert Report

"I never think of the future - it comes soon enough."

Albert Einstein
Physicist and Pacifist

40. The future is now.

 Fishtip™: Surf the web daily for at least one new, surprising thing. Keep a log and review it for potential new-business *crazy ideas*.

When I started selling the *Scream* (1991), it was a different world. Businesses communicated via hard-wired telephones, faxes and letters. International communications were faxed due to time differences. No cell phones, no Internet.

We conversed somewhat formally, as in this typical communication with my Taiwan trading partner:

> *"Dear Mr. Kang: Hello and thank you for your fax with the price quote. After I have had a chance to review the information I will get back in touch with my decision. Thank you again for your help and Best Regards…Robert"*

I still communicate this way with all of my international associates, though now through email. However, for many other transactions, that formality is history. Faster information exchange via cell phones and Internet has fostered "short hand" messages:

"Got the quote, I'll let you know."

Though they have taken some adjustment on the part of old-schoolers, these new communication technologies and styles have created amazing new opportunities, especially in the worlds of business and learning.

As more and more databases are put online in **the cloud**, astounding and ever-increasing amounts of information are accessible by anyone anywhere, and everyone everywhere. To summarize Thomas Friedman in his book, *The World is Flat*, 'In the global economy we all have equal opportunity'.

As of this writing in 2009, we google and **twitter** . Anyone can update wikipedia. Entrepreneurs are becoming **Instapreneurs** and **Intrapreneurs** . Identifying and targeting a niche market is easier than ever. Companies regularly ask customers for new-product ideas, and the public responds…what a deal! Smart phones are edging laptops and cameras as windows on the world, with more and more practical and fun, user-created apps being offered daily.

At the end of this book, you will find resources that can help you take advantage of these communication changes as you launch and grow your business. Start surfing. Tomorrow, you'll find resources that don't even exist today. So many links, so little time. Let your left brain guide you; then, listen to your right brain. Surfing the web is bound to take you to new places.

41. Business in the Internet Age

Running a successful products-based business in pre-Internet times meant attending to several things:

Generating *crazy ideas* and handling legal issues, plus marketing, sales, manufacturing, distribution, inventory, staffing, client management, cash flow…..

In the Internet Age, your products-based business may be strikingly different. You still need to hone your *crazy idea* and do thorough legal homework and negotiating, but beyond that you've got new choices. You can handle everything to make and move the physical stuff as we did, or you can run a **virtual web business** with you as an instapreneur, and never touch a product.

With **user-generated commerce**, you can outsource all the "making and moving stuff" steps, and arrange to have them done on demand:

- On demand printing on a wide variety of products, partnering with companies like CafePress.com, zazzle.com, StyleShake.com, SpreadShirt.com
- On demand books, CDs and DVDs with companies like CreateSpace.com and blurb.com
- On demand furniture, toy and jewelry manufacture with companies like ponoko.com in New Zealand
- On demand metal and fabrication with companies like emachineshop.com
- Amazon Marketplace / Amazon Virtual Domain

Though Amazon.com started out as an online book store, since 2006 Amazon has begun making its extensive resources available to companies for a variety of purposes, especially for infrastructure web services. Using Amazon Web Services (AWS) you can rent only the server space that you need and have their experts help you set up your service as well as maintain as much of its operation as you require. You could set up a truly virtual web business where all you would need would be a portal to run things. That portal could be as simple as a laptop or even a smart phone…. wildly amazing!

> *"The Internet is just a world passing around notes in a classroom."*
>
> Jon Stewart
> Comedian, political satirist
> and host of The Daily Show

42. Cyber-Sales and Marketing

With wireless communication devices and the Internet, brick and mortar stores have lost ground to people who are embracing on-line shopping: it's convenient, efficient and offers endless choices. It's no wonder then that those same stores now all have a web presence. If you don't, you're dead.

So how do you take advantage of this new landscape for sales and marketing? How can you command attention in this new environment? There are any number of books and web sites devoted entirely to using the Internet. A few tips though will get you a long way:

- First, clearly know what you are offering and explain it simply.
- Have your own website that shows what you are offering.
- Construct your website so that it rises in search results.
- Make it really easy for people to get information on your products or services, and to understand their options.
- Make it really easy for people to buy your products and services.
- Know other websites where you can promote or sell your stuff, and send them free samples for review.
- Sites like Amazon.com, eBay.com or craigslist.com can basically be extensions of your store, selling your existing merchandise.
- Sites like CafePress.com & threadless.com will help you sell your designs in their virtual stores, plus they make and stock the merchandise.
- Social Networking sites like myspace.com, facebook.com and linkedin.com will give you the opportunity to create grass roots buzz. When people like something, word spreads fast – hundreds of times faster than before.
- With that in mind, you must be 100% reliable and accountable. Social Networking speed is also used to warn people about unreliable sellers and disappointing products and services.

Even with the potential of the web, don't rule out sending information to traditional media like:

- Trade Publications
- Newspapers
- Magazines
- Radio and TV shows
- Special Events.

Remember that people still love a good story. If it's really good, the Internet will pick it up and help it along.

There are always lots of ways to spend money promoting your *crazy idea*. Just make sure you've taken advantage of the many free ones before opening up your wallet.

With Internet searches, you can identify groups of all sizes that might want to buy your *crazy idea*. Brainstorm sideways... the non-obvious will provide you with the additional income to make you a success.

To rise to the top of an Internet search without paying advertising fees, you either need to be very unique – the only place to get a particular product or service – or you need to be linked to a LOT of other websites, especially sites that have a high **Page Rank**. More precisely, you want specific pages on your site linked from other sites' pages. Sites with high Page Ranks tend to be respected, credible sites that get tons of visits, such as well known news organizations. If you are mentioned in the *New York Times*, that link will be recognized by a search engine as being important. Just having your thousand friends link to your site may not help as much to raise you in search results.

Additionally, you want a reasonable number of **Key Words** in large type, repeated on your Home Page to make it clear what you offer. For my site I have made sure to include all of the following: *Scream* inflatable (several times), frustrated, tense, therapeutic, stress-reliever, tension-reliever, art, Munch, public art, mural, speaker, motivational speaker, college, university, entrepreneur, entrepreneurial, entrepreneurism, innovation, Keynote and more. On resumes now, it is suggested to put key words within, and if you can't put them in, just to add a line in tiny type at the end that says: keywords: xxxx. The parallel would be a paragraph on your homepage that could be read or skipped, but has all the keywords. The idea is that you don't just say "Welcome," or "Home Page."

On the Internet, marketing and selling are more blended than in the "real world," Of course, you still need to market (create a buzz about you or your products) before someone will be interested enough to buy what you are selling.

In marketing and advertising, repetition and constancy are what keeps you in the minds of the buying public. One-time events, though glamorous and potentially attention-getting, can be missed; but that little weekly classified ad or pop-up or Google Ad Word will eventually be seen by a LOT of people.

David Seaman, the author of the informative and fun to read book, *Dirty Little Secrets of Buzz, How to Attract Massive Attention to Your Business, Your Product or Yourself*, understands how things have changed with the Internet, especially in the last few years:

"With Facebook and MySpace, it's fundamentally different now. It only takes 20 seconds for somebody to post a link to your blog and share it with 2,000 people that they know. And in turn, some percentage of those 2,000, the content may resonate with them, they may enjoy it and they're going to do the same thing, and it's just going to spread in a matter of hours. It used to be you had to be a big Website, or you had to have a big link on CNN.com or major news sites to create that kind of buzz, and now you don't have to do that anymore."

Based on this, make sure you take advantage of the Internet with social networking services, blogs and of course, a dynamite website of your own, overflowing with free content. Most of these suggestions can be very low cost and very high impact. Use them or you will never even make it on the radar.

Be forewarned, though, that all of these sites have etiquette and rules, sometimes unwritten, and these expected behaviors differ from site to site. With millions of people using these sites, you'll get differing opinions about what is OK and what is not OK to do. Just take some time to get a lay of the land. Participate as a non-demanding equal, see if what you want to do is appropriate and then slowly introduce yourself and your offering. You have as good a chance at success as the next person.

As conventional stores loose their grip on the marketplace, and people get more comfortable shopping online, millions of businesses are setting up shop on the web. Specialty sites like Cafe-Press.com, threadless.com and etsy.com offer not just an array of user-designed goods to buy, but they offer an opportunity for you to sell your own creations; in fact, that is how they survive and grow. They want you…so, what are you waiting for?

"I feel I'm able to serve my customer by knowing what she or he wants. One of the ways I'm able to do this is through my website, and email: people give me great ideas, tell me what they want, what they don't want. It's really instrumental, and helps me stay in touch with people."

Kathy Ireland
*Former model, CEO and Designer
of her brand product marketing
company, Kathy Ireland Worldwide*

43. Extreme Creativity

 Fishtip™: Be an artist in your approach to life. If you look at everything as if it has some other purpose, you'll discover it.

 Fishtip™: What is unique about you or what you do? Is it worth sharing with the world?

 Fishtip™: What resource or diversion do you think everyone needs on their smart phone? Can you sell 10,000 of them? Find someone to help you make it happen.

Two of the more well-known and amazing things happening in early 2009 in the world of innovation and creativity are found at You Tube and the Apple App Store. Both are drawing on the unlimited potential of people around the world to create content. Both have gone way beyond what the creators envisioned. Sure, a lot of YouTube is barely watchable. But the stuff that shines through is gold....literally. In fact, the folks at Google will partner with you and share ad revenues if you:

1) Create original videos suitable for online streaming

2) Own the copyrights and distribution rights for all audio and video content that you upload -- no exceptions.

3) Regularly upload videos that are viewed by thousands of YouTube users

Google doesn't have to do anything but pick and choose from an endlessly growing pool of submissions from very creative folks. To learn more, surf http://www.youtube.com/partners

Similarly, those really smart people at Apple are allowing – encouraging – anyone to create applications for the iPhone and iTouch. If Apple accepts your app, they make it available at the iTunes Store. There are thousands already available, You can offer yours for free or charge for it. Most apps go for $0.99. The developer gets 70%, Apple 30%. Once you develop the application, there is no cost to you unless you make improvements: what a deal. Several developers have netted hundreds of thousands of dollars from their 70%. One company, smule.com, has made over a million dollars. The most popular apps can sell 10,000 units, a day! I introduced my first one in early 2009, Cat Purr. Are you working on yours yet?

- For information on what apps are currently available go to the Apple iTunes Store.

- To look into creating your own iPhone app, go to http://developer.apple.com/iphone/

All those Apple apps show that talent is out there to create content ranging from very practical, to purely entertaining, to aesthetically mind-boggling. And Apple didn't have to hire any of those developers. All they said was, "Wanna have some fun and make some money?"

Well.......YEAH!

It's that tradition of innovation in a new form, the same spirit that fueled the individuals who invented cars, telescopes, planes, radios, computers and more. It's the same burning vision that inspires artists and performers of all types to constantly reinterpret experience and push the limits of what we know as art. If only more corporations, governments and organizations would use this same strategy to encourage and support hundreds of thousands of garage inventors, classroom motivators (read: teachers), artists, even the employees in their own companies (what a simple radical idea!), many seemingly insurmountable problems would be well on the way to being solved. And that doesn't even take into account all of the breakthroughs that would be simultaneously discovered and developed 'off to the side'.

If you are a manager or CEO or any other kind of decision maker, ask yourself this: "What am I doing to promote innovation?"

> *"Imagination is more important than knowledge..."*
>
> Albert Einstein

> *"Well, when you're trying to create things that are new, you have to be prepared to be on the edge of risk."*
>
> Michael Eisner
> *Entertainment Executive, Former CEO of Walt Disney Corporation*

> *"Innovation distinguishes between a leader and a follower."*
>
> Steve Jobs
> *Chairman, CEO & Co-founder of Apple, Inc.*

Selling The Scream

44. Creativity Blasts

Here are a few of my favorite websites for when I want a triple expresso of creativity:

www.burningman.com
Grandpappy of all artsy festivals

www.oobjets.com
Collections of manmade stuff, amazing

www.designboom.com
A web site focused on contemporary design whose mission includes enriching the dialogue between the worlds of design, creative professionals, industry and society….in short, lots of very cool stuff.

www.collegedegrees.com/blog/2008/06/11/100-useful-web-tools-for-writers
Tools to free up writer's blocks, plus way more

www.instructables.com/home
How to make loads of cool stuff

www.makerfaire.com
Garage inventor meets the Renaissance

www.steampunkworkshop.com
Basement tinkerer meets Victorian punk

www.boingboing.net
Directory of wonderful things

http://jeff560.tripod.com/words.html
A Collection of Word Oddities and Trivia, isn't language amazing?

www.nullsleep.com/index.php
Edgy music from game devices

www.secondlife.com
Avatars and more

www.mamalisa.com
Amazing kid's storytelling site

www.thetanknyc.org/contact
Cool performance space

www.oddmusic.com
Weird instruments galore

www.windworld.com
Experimental musical instruments

http://video.scifi.com/player/?id=224004#videoid=865162
Battle Star Galactica: What the Frak? A hilarious idea on how to
summarize a story; it may give you an idea for creating your *crazy
Idea's* mythology. ...OK, I'm a fan!

Take Action!

▶ What can you gather and offer that will attract a large web
population? If it's cool enough, if it has real value, if it is
more than just surface facts, you'll become famous.

45. So, what are you waiting for?

Remember when you were a kid and you decided to finally go off the high dive? You were excitedly waiting on line with your friends who had already done it…they didn't seem nervous at all. Then it was your turn to climb the ladder. You looked up. It was tall but it didn't seem all that bad. Half way up the ladder though it began to grow more and more steps until by the time you got to the top it was the tallest thing around and at least a hundred feet down to the water.

You watched the person in front of you charge off the end of the board screaming and fall forever until they cannon balled into the pool.

You were told to wait until they came up before taking your turn. But why were they still under water? Did something go wrong? Were they all right? Were they drowning? Finally they appeared, smiling…huh!

OK, you can do it. Walk to the end. But the farther out you go the more the world around you bounces up and down. You pull your arms into your chest and feel your heart beating like it's going to burst right out of you. This is crazy. Why oh why did you climb that ladder?

You turn and see kids all the way down to the ground, looking at you like, "OK, jump already!"

You are scared but know you can't go back down. You look at the water, at the line of kids, out at the adults sitting in their chairs, at the water again and slowly take the last steps to the end of the board and then someone behind you shouts, "Jump" and you obey, leaping up and out. For a moment you are motionless and weightless and then you begin to fall down but the illusion is that everything else is going up and it all turns blurry and you hear someone screaming and then you realize it's you and after forever there is a loud Splash! as you hit the water and you go under and then all is suddenly silent…….you open your eyes to a million bubbles through which you see phantom shapes in the distance… it's wonderfully warm and comforting. Then you realize you are alive and need air and rise to the surface to breathe. You swim to the side of the pool where a waiting friend asks "So, how was it?", to which you automatically reply, "That was great, let's do it again!"

You are fearless and now you can do anything.

Remember this: it doesn't matter if you are thinking about a product, a service or an innovation within a company. By having confidence in yourself, by valuing your dream, by finding the right assistance you too can begin the process of making your own *crazy idea* a reality. Sound good? Ready? JUMP!

46. Your Turn

It's been a while since we first talked about taking your *crazy idea* and heading down the entrepreneurial path. Having shown you how I learned tons and made millions, it's now your turn.

Let the stories and Secrets, the Fishtips™ and Lessons Learned, the bumps and Action Steps percolate in your brain as you ponder which of your *crazy ideas* to sculpt into a business.

Look all around; don't always follow the obvious path.

Let the ups and downs prepare you for the unexpected. Surrender.

Let yourself see mistakes as opportunities for growth and innovation.

Let yourself be helped, because all you have to do us ask.

And let yourself be successful, wildly, amazingly, astonishingly wonderfully, successful. It all starts with you.

> *"A real entrepreneur is somebody who has no safety net underneath them."*
>
> Henry Kravis
> *Business financier and investor*

> *"Life is either a daring adventure, or nothing."*
>
> Helen Keller
> *Author, political activist and lecturer*

Selling The Scream

Resources

While traveling the ups and downs and bumps in the Entrepreneurial road, it would be good to have an emergency tool box…that would be this resource section. Consisting of web resources of both the practical and whimsical, and topped off with some books to peruse and an extensive Glossary, you should feel more confident when you walk out the door tomorrow and announce to the world:

I have *crazy ideas*!
I Can Do This!
People Will Help Me!

Selling The Scream

47. Internet Resources

The following are some well-trafficked sites currently offering valuable services to entrepreneurs and instapreneurs and intrapreneurs. I take no compensation from these sites (except my own!), though I do access some to help me with my own business. How or if you use them is entirely up to you, and I do not guarantee any degree of success in your business ventures by my mentioning them here. For any one of these, there are likely a dozen or a hundred or a thousand other sites offering similar and competitive information and services. It's up to you to choose.

One of the great assets of the web is that sites are expected to accept and post user feedback. This provides all of us with first-hand evaluations. It started with people leaving feedback about eBay traders, and now it's everywhere. If a site or service is great, we'll find out. If a site or service is shady, it won't last long: word spreads really fast online. Good Luck!

NOTE: Resources and Glossary terms are current as of date of publication. The reader assumes all risk of using these resources and is encouraged to check all resources and any pertinent Glossary terms for accuracy. Companies go through changes and the Internet evolves constantly.

www.robertfishbone.com My website. Find out about my speaker programs for corporations, colleges & universities and arts associations, read my blog, download free articles, take a mural tour, peruse and contribute to the *Screameria*, check out my You Tube videos and order my cool stuff: this book, *Scream* inflatables & keychains, my CD of music and storytelling, Magic Cubes, Thunder Tubes™ & Washboard Ties™.

www.sarahlinquist.com Extensive photographs of our mural work can be found on my wife's web site. Check it out!

www.grotro.com Trophy Music Company, the distributors of my line of novelty percussion instruments; contact them to buy a single item, or to see about setting up a wholesale account.

http://archon.mohistory.org/controlcard. php?id=2045 Our mural archives from 1974-1993, housed at the Missouri Historical Society Museum. You need to visit to see it all...it takes up eleven cubic feet, plus designs and film/video.

www.sba.gov The website of the US Small Business Administration has programs and services to help you start, grow and succeed in business. It also has information about domestic and international regulations, plus potential sources for funding assistance. An amazing resource.

www.StartRunGrow.com A non-governmental site with thousands of free pages of advice on starting, running and growing your business – more info than you can imagine.

www.entrepreneur.com The web site of *Entrepreneur Magazine* which is a publication that carries news stories about entrepreneurialism, small business management, and business opportunities. *Entrepreneur* also publishes books for small business people, through its Entrepreneur Press division, featuring a backlist of over 200 titles in categories such as franchising, wealth building, startups, sales and marketing and home businesses. This web site is a treasure chest of current information.

www.entrepreneur.com/startingabusiness/business-plans/article38308-1.html Detailed outline of the elements of a formal business plan.

www.yellow-tie.net A non-profit organization run by volunteers who are dedicated to helping businesspeople build the relationships they need to generate stratospheric success. A great resource.

www.careerbuilder.com Largest and most successful of all the online job seeker/finder sites in the United States with over 20 million unique visitors each month. It provides online career search services for more than 1,900 partners as of March, 2008, including 140 newspapers and portals such as America Online and MSN. They offer a host of job search tools including help with resumes.

www.score.org The Service Corps of Retired Executives, a nonprofit resource for small businesses made up of 11,200 volunteers across the country who have been in your shoes. They are successful entrepreneurs and executives who love business and want to share their knowledge with you, so you can live your dream.

www.eLance.com An exchange place for people offering professional services, and prospective clients seeking that expertise.

www.woopidoo.com Motivational business portal from Villanova University. Includes a lot of inspirational business quotations.

www.bnet.com/2403-13070_23-196888.html Stories of Intrapreneurship

www.bnet.com/2403-13070_23-196890.html More stories of Intrapreneurship

www.lemonadeday.org Lemonade Day is designed to teach young people how to start, own and operate their own lemonade business. On Lemonade Day, thousands of kids set up Lemonade stands across a number of US cities. During this process, young students learn about budgets, securing investors, identifying retail locations, advertising and making money. They also learn character-building lessons such as customer service, saving money and giving back to the community.

❂ ❂ ❂

On-Demand Providers

 Fishtip: Though on-demand providers help you establish an instant business, you will still need to drive traffic to your site, whether it is your own site, or a gallery hosted with an on-demand site.

Use email campaigns and newsletters, connections through social networking sites, and web media mentions that will get search engines to notice you. Make sure your site is attractive and really easy to understand and navigate, and makes it easy for people to buy your stuff. Don't be afraid to recommend someone else's site either; the good deed will be repaid.

www.cafepress.com One of the most popular sites that features on-demand printing. Use on-demand printing to create a revenue stream via products you may already have. From their website:

"CafePress is a community of 6.5 million members, where folks from all walks of life gather online to create, sell, and buy T-Shirts and other "print-on-demand" products (it's called user-generated commerce, and we're the leader in it). Our Shopkeepers offer over 150 million products-including everything from funny T-Shirts to custom hats, hoodies, mugs, and more. With so many choices, CafePress is a great place to find gift Ideas for personalized gifts and one-of-kind gear. If you can't find the perfect design, simply create your own custom T-Shirts or even custom embroidery. Rewarding self-expressionists since 1999, CafePress is based in San Mateo, CA."

www.spoonflower.com Design your own fabric and then purchase it in quantities as small as a fat quarter and as large as yards. The price is about double that of good cottons sold retail.

www.threadless.com Threadless is a community-centered online apparel store run by skinnyCorp of Chicago, Illinois, since 2000. They also have two brick and mortar stores in Chicago. Co-founders Jake Nickell and Jacob DeHart started the company with $1,000 in seed money after entering an Internet t-shirt design contest. Members of the Threadless community submit t-shirt designs online; the designs are then put to a public vote who score them on a scale of 0-5. On average, around 700 designs compete in any given week. Each week, the staff selects about ten designs. Each designer selected receives $2,000 in cash, as well as an additional $500 for every reprint. This is a great model of using your customers to build all aspects of your business and have a lot of fun doing, and another opportunity to create a revenue stream… check out their website.

www.ponoko.com This New Zealand based company will custom make certain types of furniture, toys and jewelry out of wood and plastic; just email or fax them your design. Like with Café Press, a customer can browse your gallery and choose a design. The people at Ponoko will fabricate it, ship it to the client and send you your royalty. Sweet.

www.createspace.com An on-demand site for printing books and burning/producing CDs and DVDs.

www.instantpublisher.com Since self publishing has come into play as one of the major alternatives out there for writers who want to publish a book, a number of companies now offer afford-able book publishing services to individuals in quantities as little as 25 books. Instantpublisher has a unique transfer software that allows individuals to submit their books from any manuscript layout software they use, and send it directly from their desktop. Instant-publisher will then publish a book in trade quality from 25 to 5,000 copies in less than 7-10 working days depending on options. This book was printed with an on-demand shop, Mira Digital Publishing in St. Louis, MO.

www.emachineshop.com Provides convenient, low-cost fabrication of a broad range of custom parts and products in metal and plastics. Create what you once thought impossible.

www.etsy.com Etsy is the online marketplace for buying and selling all things handmade. They connect buyers with indepen-dent creators and shop owners to find the very best in handmade, vintage and supplies. I have friends who offer their crafts on etsy.

www.inventbay.com A popular site for inventors and for investors looking for opportunities. Lots of information about the entire process of bringing your invention to the marketplace includ-ing intellectual property protection such as patents.

www.apple.com/iPhone If you've never seen an iPhone, you've at least heard of it. One very cool feature is iPhone Apps: Apple created a software developer's kit for independent devel-opers, and there are now thousands of applications available for the iPhone – games, utilities, lifestyle diversions, databases and web-connected services… Truly amazing. Most apps sell for $.99 or $1.99; many are free. This is a place to see grassroots, cutting age creativity. It's a new opportunity to create revenue streams for yourself. The first app I created for the iPhone is called Cat Purr.

www.youtube.com Like many web ventures, what began as a small operation has rapidly blossomed into a worldwide phenomena. Not only is You Tube a place to post your family's movies, you can now earn money by becoming a partner. If you can generate your own content, if it's all your own, original material and if you get thousands of views a week, You Tube will consider placing ads on your website, and will share in those revenues. Brilliant.

www.craigslist.com The place to buy and sell goods and services for free, especially locally – no shipping to deal with. It's the dominant way, nationally, to rent property. This new model for commerce is a major, direct challenge to newspaper classifieds and to Internet giants like eBay and Amazon. I use it often to buy and sell. Simple and easy.

www.ebay.com The original powerhouse of auction sites, now going through changes because of places like craigslist. Has helped many people clear out their basements and garages and fill them back up again. Many people support themselves through ebay sales.

www.amazon.com A one-stop website for buying and selling new and used items, especially books, music, movies and electronics. Amazon realized they could minimize any threat posed by competitors by allowing them to sell directly through the Amazon website. Like Lincoln bringing the opposition into his cabinet, at least Amazon keeps tabs on what the competition is doing, and Amazon makes a percentage of everything sold through its site. Smart.

www.aws.amazon.com Amazon has so many servers and so much hard disc space that they rent it out. You can set up an entire web-based business using their support structure. You work with the folks at Amazon to create exactly what you need.

Amazon's rented servers are one puff of a new business model, The Cloud. "The Cloud" refers to everybody's data on all those storage devices, floating in cyberspace, not sitting on our desks; the term "The Cloud," is an abstraction for the complex infrastructure it conceals. With Amazon Web Services and other major server rental sites, all of your data is stored remotely, maybe even in multiple locations. The parts of your business that required you to own computers and software can now be handled by a third party. You may not need an office or warehouse other than your laptop or even just your smart phone; no more systems to buy, lease or maintain. No utility bills for running and cooling computers, no technicians to hire. "The Cloud" is astonishing, and like many of these listings, and real clouds, it changes constantly.

www.wired.com One of the first magazines devoted to the Internet and all forms of electronic devices and communications. A great magazine and a great site to get information on what is cutting edge today – and what may be coming tomorrow.

www.free-legal-document.com In addition to supplying a wide range of free legal documents and forms, also advises and notes what to look out for before you sign.

www.legaldocs.com Helps you prepare customized legal documents and forms online; fees charged.

Selling The Scream

48. Print on Paper: Still Great

The Thesaurus: A Time-Tested Tool for Sparking Creativity

Find what you're not looking for.

Sure, it's easy to just ask your electronic thesaurus for synonyms when you've used that same word already. But by going the electronic route, you miss the serendipity of adjacent words that have absolutely nothing to do with your current quest. You do find a synonym, but pass by the opportunity to discover something new. It is the surprise of what you are not looking for that holds the key to creative thinking and innovation.

In *A Whack on the Side of The Head*, a wonderful and time-tested book on unlocking creativity, Roger von Oech makes this point again and again:

"When you are trying to develop new ideas…narrowing your focus and limiting your field of view…may prevent you from looking in outside areas for ideas. Develop the explorer's attitude, the outlook that wherever you go there are ideas waiting to be discovered….allow yourself to be led astray. If you discover something anomalous or unusual, use it as a stepping stone to something unexpected", and, *"Discovery consists of looking at the same thing as everyone else and thinking something different."*

In short, don't be afraid to wander around and peek under things. If you're lucky, you'll get bitten with a new idea.

Read the newsPAPER

Experience the news with your emotions, your body and all your senses, not just your brain.

Paper vs. online thesaurus is the difference between analog and digital. While digital is efficient and quick, it can also be pretty linear and one-dimensional. One of my favorite examples of this analog-digital difference is the newspaper. When I look at the paper online, I lose out on the 3D, physical experience of glancing around at the other stories on the page. Reading a physical newspaper, my whole body is involved: where and how I sit, how I move my arms as I turn and fold the pages, the sound, smell and texture of the paper. Reading it online robs you of that body experience; you respond more mentally than emotionally to the content.

Computer and TV screens make us lose out on real life, too. They flatten out everything so that there is a sameness to the content. Little wonder that movies, TV shows and the news look a little bit too similar to each other. Sure, digital is convenient and fast, and we all use it. Just make sure you mix it with things you hold in your hands that reflect light, not just screens that transmit it.

Read books

OK, listen to books if you want, but digest them: great stuff.

Business-related books

- Growing Your Business by Mark LeBlanc. Wonderful and comprehensive in its simplicity, Marc gives you tools to make manageable steps in daily and month long intervals. Why wait a year?

- Make a Name for Yourself by Scott Ginsberg, the "Nametag Guy." A book that is fun to read and creatively designed, it provides tools on ways to make yourself stand out and be remembered. Scott's style of writing proves that the medium is the message.

- Made to Stick: Why Some Ideas Survive and Others Die by Chip Heath and Dan Heath. Using the acronym SUCCES, the Heaths explain how to make your ideas effective, compelling and memorable. Although aimed at a business audience, the authors' suggestions for effective communication can also be useful for a variety of classroom activities and creative endeavors.

- The Acorn Principal by Jim Cathcart. A guide to finding out how "rich, full and rewarding your life can be." Jim says, *"We have three roles here on earth: to learn, to love and to live. When we stop learning, we start to stagnate and die. When we stop loving, we lose our sense of purpose and become self-centered. When we stop*

living, we deny the world the benefits of our talents."
Jim's book helps to identify blocks to growth and explains how to nurture the giant, deep-rooted oak within. A time tested classic.

- <u>Dirty Little Secrets of Buzz</u> by David Seaman. The subtitle says it all; How to Attract Massive Attention for Your Business, Your Product or Yourself. What's really great is that David is very familiar with social networking media and using the Internet to your advantage. Chock full of useful, usable tips, many of them free or very low cost.

Creativity related books

- <u>A Whack on the Side of Your Head</u> by Roger von Oech. Since its publication in 1983, this book has proven to help people understand and remove mental blocks, break habits and old patterns, and shift focus to open new ways of thinking, and it's fun!

- <u>Thinkertoys</u> by Michael Michalko. This book shows through numerous analogies, stories, quotations, games, tricks and exercises, all fun, that by changing your perspectives, you can expand your possibilities. Like "A Whack...", another standard in the creative arsenal.

- <u>The Truth About Chuck Norris</u> by Ian Spector, an example of a website gone wild, with the content dreamed up by the public. It shows that given the right challenge and a good theme, people will break down your door to participate and prove that their creative ideas know no end.

Books worth re-reading

I've read them all more than once and expect to read them again.

- <u>Tales of a Dalai Lama</u> by Pierre DeLattre. Stories based on what might have been going on in the Potala in Tibet... an imaginative romp through the spiritual and mundane.

- <u>Snow Crash</u> by Neal Stephenson. A not so hard to believe look at the not so distant future where America is known for two things: software development and on-time pizza delivery, and where the Internet has become the Metaverse which is populated by Avatars, fantastical simulations of ourselves...why not? Ever heard of SecondLife.com?

- <u>eat, love, pray</u> by Elizabeth Gilbert. Subtitled " One Woman's Search for Everything Across Italy, India and Indonesia," her combination of storytelling, creative language and fearlessness make the lessons learned precious gifts we are lucky to receive.

Glossary

Terms highlighted in the text, plus a few more.

Accounts payable: What you owe to someone else.

Accounts receivable: What someone else owes you.

Air freight: Shipping goods via airplane. A less expensive alternative than standard UPS or Fedex.

Angel funding: Money provided by an angel investor or angel, an affluent individual who provides capital for a business start-up, usually in exchange for convertible debt or ownership equity. A small but increasing number of angel investors organize themselves into angel groups or angel networks to share research and pool their investment capital.

Artist Rights Society: Artists Rights Society (ARS) is the preeminent copyright, licensing, and monitoring organization for visual artists in the United States. Founded in 1987, ARS represents the intellectual property rights interests of over 50,000 visual artists and estates of visual artists from around the world (painters, sculptors, photographers, architects and others). www.arsny.com

B2B: Business to business. Businesses doing business with other businesses, for mutual benefit.

Bill of lading: A document issued by the carrier acknowledging that specified goods have been received on board as cargo for conveyance to a specified location for delivery to a specified party.

Blog: A contraction of the term weblog, is a website usually maintained by an individual with regular entries of commentary, descriptions of events, or other material such as graphics or video. "Blog" can also be used as a verb, meaning to maintain or add content to a blog. Some blogs have massive followings and can influence opinion, while others are written for self satisfaction. As of March, 2009, there are currently over 100,000,000 blogs.

BONO: An independent Norwegian copyright organisation that manages the rights of visual artists pursuant to the Norwegian

Copyright Act. BONO enters into agreements regarding the use of visual art, and collects remuneration on behalf of its members. Another important aspect of BONO's activities is informing members and users about copyright in the area of visual art. BONO works with sister organizations in many other countries. www.bono.no/html/english/english_intro.html

Brainstorm: (v) To generate ideas solo or in a group, with no first-round evaluation as to merit or feasibility. (n) An innovative idea generated in a brainstorm session.

Business plan: Steps necessary to accomplish your business goal. Used to complete the process and/or to measure results and make adjustments during the process.

Buyer's insurance: Protects you in case something happens to your goods in shipment or in storage.

CD: The finance kind. not the music kind…. A Certificate of Deposit is an investment with an amount, a set interest rate and a set payment date.

Cancel date: The date at which an order is cancelled. Stores often state the cancel date on an order. In other words, if you can't deliver by the pre-arranged date, they don't have to buy the stuff. Pay attention to the cancel date!

Capitalization: Putting up the necessary funds to start or maintain a business, often for a new venture.

Chinese New Year (CNY): Yearly celebration. Chinese factories are closed one to two weeks. No matter what.

Check with your factory and shipper and plan accordingly.

Year	Start of CNY	Year of the
2009 - Jan. 26		Ox
2010 - Feb. 14		Tiger
2011 - Feb. 3		Rabbit
2012 - Jan. 23		Dragon
2013 – Feb. 10		Snake
2014 – Jan. 31		Horse

Selling The Scream

2015 – Feb.19	Sheep
2016 – Feb. 8	Monkey
2017 – Jan. 28	Rooster
2018 – Feb. 16	Dog

"The Cloud": Network of the world's electronic storage devices and all the data on them, more commonly referred to as the Internet.

Cloud Computing: The ability to upload all types of files to to online storage servers and then access them from any Internet connected portal.

COD (see oh dee, not a fish): Cash on delivery. You must pay for the goods before the delivery service will release them to you. Often used with UPS or Fedex.

Commercial invoice: Shows the value of the shipment, usually your cost. If you are drop shipping products directly to your client, the invoice needs to show their cost, not yours.

Credit Union: A credit union is a cooperative financial institution that is owned and controlled by its members, and operated for the purpose of promoting thrift, providing credit at reasonable rates, and providing other financial services to its members. Many credit unions exist to further community development or sustainable international development on a local level. A viable alternative to loans from banks especially in times of a financial downturn.

Customs brokerage forms: Documents required by the importing country to determine what taxes and duties may be charged.

Cut-out: A shape cut in silhouette from flat material, like a paper doll. Ours were cut from 4' x 8' sheets of plywood and Sintra™ plastic.

Death & Taxes™: A poster designed by Jess Bachman giving a striking visual representation of how tax dollars are allocated and spent. Available at www.wallstats.com/deathandtaxes

DACS and sister organizations: Design and Artists Copyright Society, located in the UK. They help to monitor illegal use of artists' copyrighted materials. Sister organizations exist in most other countries. With a harmonized copyright system, they help each other protect the artists' rights.

Dating: Setting payment timetables. Once you sell something, you want to get paid. Businesses with a good record for paying their bills often don't have to pay right away; instead, they have "terms." Terms are often Net 15 or Net 30, meaning the bill has to be paid in 15 or 30 days from delivery of the goods or service. Terms are sometimes longer, even Net 45 or 60, especially in Q4. This gives companies extra time to make their holiday sales. But it also means you are out your money that much longer. Be careful. To encourage clients to pay early, discounts are sometimes offered.

Disaster and Inventory Insurance: Talk to an insurance agent to see what types of coverage you may need. How valuable and irreplaceable are your office contents and your inventory? Are they all in one location? Are you protected against fire, flood, theft and other natural disaster? You'll need to balance the cost of insurance with the potential benefits it provides in case of a loss. There was once a fire in the floor above our warehouse space and there was a lot of water damage to our inventory of Van Gogh poster games. Our insurance covered us for the loss.

Drop ship: Send goods directly to your clients, sometimes from your factory, sometimes from your shipping facility. Third parties, like Internet resellers, will sometimes ask if you can drop ship to individuals who buy from them. If you choose to do this, they understand you would add a charge on to process the order. It is a great deal for them, as they then do not have to handle the products at all, just list them on their web site and handle the transaction. We never offered this service.

Entrepreneur: Someone who sees an opportunity and is willing to take upon her/himself a new venture or enterprise and accepts full responsibility for the outcome. Entrepreneurship is often a difficult undertaking, as a vast majority of new businesses fail. Entrepreneurship ranges from solo projects to major undertakings. Many "high-profile" entrepreneurial ventures seek Venture Capital or Angel Funding in order to raise capital to build the business. Angel investors generally seek returns of 20-30% and more extensive involvement in the business.

Fair use: A doctrine in United States Copyright law that allows limited use of copyrighted material without requiring permission from the rights holders, such as use for scholarship or review. It provides for the legal, non-licensed citation or incorporation of copyrighted material in another author's work under a four-factor test. However, like most legal issues, it can be a very gray area.

Footprint: The area something takes up on a flat surface.

Fung Shui: An ancient Chinese system of aesthetics believed to use the laws of both heaven and earth to receive positive life energy and thus improve ones life. Fung Shui often relates to direction and placement of furniture, mirrors, and windows in one's home or office.

Fulfillment House: A facility that can warehouse your inventory, and take and process orders. Their fee is often based on the number of orders they will have to deal with, and how much work will be involved in picking, packing and shipping each order. Accounts Payable and Receivable are usually left to you.

Google: Started as an Internet search engine, many consider it to be the most powerful brand in the world. Also a verb describing a search on the Internet. For more information, just google Google. The name is derived from the mathematical term google, which is a one followed by 100 zeroes…that's a lot of stuff!

Google Ad Words: A way to advertise on Google's search engine. AdWords offers pay-per-click (PPC) advertising, and site-targeted advertising for both text and banner ads. The AdWords program includes local, national, and international distribution. Advertisers specify the words that should trigger their ads and the maximum amount they are willing to pay per click. When a user searches Google's search engine for relevant words, their ads are shown as "sponsored links" on the right side of the screen, and sometimes above the main search results.

Idea Bounce Both a web site and a competition developed by the Skandalaris Center for Entrepreneurial Studies at Washington University in St. Louis, Missouri. It provides resources and networking opportunities for creators, inventors, implementers, investors, business people, artists, service providers, customers, mentors, and others - the web of innovators who transform ideas into reality, create value and bring inventions to market. See full details at http://sces.wustl.edu/ideabounce/

Instapreneurs: Individuals who make use of on-demand, web-based resources to create businesses in which they do not need to maintain any of the physical facilities normally associated with running a business; thus involving much less risk than a normal, capitalized venture.

Intrapreneurs: Individuals looking for ways to innovate within an existing company, think in-house entrepreneur.

Key Words: A term, or multiple terms that capture the essence of the topic of a document. Careful choice and placement can help your document (or web site) rise to the top in a web search.

Lamarr, Hedy: Silver Screen superstar of the 1930's and 40's (born Hedwig Kiesler Markey) who, with the help of composer George Antheil invented a secret communication system in an effort to help the allies defeat the Germans in World War II. The invention, patented in 1941, manipulated radio frequencies between transmission and reception to develop an unbreakable code so that top-secret messages could not be intercepted. The technology, called spread spectrum, now takes on many forms. In fact, all of the spread spectrum that we use today including cell phone technology directly or indirectly flows from the invention created by Lamarr. Who knew?

Line of credit: An account via which a bank agrees to lend you money, up to a certain amount. You can borrow from that account to buy inventory or equipment, thus freeing up your other funds to run day-to-day business operations. You usually must pay off the loan to a zero balance at least once a year.

LCL: Less than a Container Load. Goods travel overseas on container ships. If you are ordering a small quantity of goods, or if the goods are small, they will only take up a portion of a 20 ft. or 40 ft. long container. When the containers arrive in your country, and after they have cleared customs, the goods are separated for delivery to various locations.

LTL: Less than a Truck Load. See LCL. Your goods are shipped on a truck along with others' goods.

Luck: Opportunity meeting passion and preparation.

Magic Cube: An item that Fishbone reinvented as a high quality museum gift. Originally sold as a premium or tourist souvenir, it is a small cube that at first looks like a version of the Rubik's Cube; but it is not. A Magic Cube is made of eight smaller cubes hinged in a clever way that allows it to be continuously opened and folded, revealing 3-6 surprise images on the inside, in addition to the six on the outside.

Mentor: An experienced person who helps you learn the ropes, often for free. You are expected to eventually mentor someone else.

MOQ: Minimum Ordering Quantity. A factory requires a minimum whenever it produces a product. This is how they make it cost effective for them and for you.

Multiple Revenue Streams: Having a variety of ways to create income from the same product or products is an effective strategy for making money. This might mean positioning your *crazy idea* for different markets, licensing it to another company, or even creating a service out of a product (being the expert). Multiple revenue streams can also mean smaller incomes from a variety of unrelated ventures. This is often the case with self employed individuals where the mantra might be, "whatever it takes".

Munch, Edvard: (1863 –1944) A Norwegian Symbolist painter, printmaker, and an important forerunner of expressionistic art. His best-known composition, *"The Scream,"* is one of the pieces in a series titled *"The Frieze of Life,"* in which Munch explored the themes of life, love, fear, death, and melancholy.

Munch Estate: The creative works of most deceased artists are controlled by estates that may consist of family members, an organization, a museum or even a municipality. In the case of Edvard Munch, it was a combination of these. To get a license to use the work of an artist, one must usually work through an organization such as BONO in Norway, DACS in the UK or the Artist Rights Society in the US.

Murals: Literally, painted artwork on a wall, found in cultures all over the world. The oldest are the cave paintings in France and Spain, and petroglyphs in Australia. Modern outdoor mural painting evolved as a way to both improve the urban landscape and communicate social messages to local populations.

The Museum Company: For a number of years, a very successful company that sold museum-related merchandise in mall shops. With 99 stores, they were our largest single client, until they went bankrupt, owing us a sizable chunk of change. Ouch!

Nature Company Stores: A chain of 114 mall stores. They offered a wide variety of goods relating to the natural world. Bought by the Discovery Channel in 1996.

Network: A system of interconnected parts or people that rely on each other and make use of each other.

Niche market: A section of the general marketplace usually defined by a specific, common interest. With the web, it has become very easy to identify and target a niche market for an ad or sales campaign.

Non-compete: An agreement that stipulates that for some period of time, one party will not go into the same business as another.

Non-disclosure agreement: A legal agreement to keep shared information secret. Often created when companies are in discussions about buyouts, or when someone wants to get quotes on a new item.

Ocean freight: Shipping goods overseas on a large container ship.

On demand: Goods made as needed, in whatever quantity needed, often with a very low minimum production run. Different from traditional manufacturing in which you may need to buy hundreds or thousands of something to make your cost manageable and your sales profitable.

Orphan Works Act of 2008 As of 05/09, this pending legislation addresses copyrighted works whose owners may be impossible to identify and locate. There is both a Senate and House version of this bill. Concerns had been raised that the uncertainty surrounding ownership of such works might needlessly discourage subsequent creators and users from incorporating such works in new creative efforts, or from making such works available to the public. On the other hand, it puts new burdens on artists to register their works. Go to www.copyright.gov/orphan/ for some governmental information, Google Orphan Works to read up on the discussion.

Packing Slip: Paper listing what's in the boxes that are being shipped. It does NOT list the value of the contents.

Pallets: Frames on which goods are stored, moved and shipped. Also called skids, they can be made of wood or other materials.

PageRank: A system designed and patented by Google to decide how important any page is on the Internet. PageRank results from a "ballot" among all the other pages on the World Wide Web, which relates to not just how many other pages yours is linked to, but how important they themselves are. In other words, if your web site is mentioned by major news organizations, that will carry a lot more weight than if your cousin likes it.

PO/purchase order: A document you create when you order something from another company or others order from you. It basically lists the parties, a description of the goods, costs and dates.

Premium/promotional item: Items given away by companies to promote their goods or services. Example: A pen or a mug with the company name on it.

Price Point: The point at which the actual price of an item is lower than its perceived value, meaning, "what a deal!".

Q4: The fourth quarter of the calendar year.

Sales representative/manufacturer's representative:
An individual, sales agency or company that sells a manufacturer's products to wholesale and retail customers. Note that manufacturer can mean the actual factory, the individual or group hiring the factory or more likely, a wholesale distributor, which is what I am. When a manufacturer hires a manufacturer's rep, this usually means that a contract is signed between the two companies, empowering the rep to sell the manufacturer's products as an agent in a defined territory. The products are usually ordered directly from the manufacturer, who then pays a sales commission to the manufacturer's rep firm. The commission rate varies according to the market and the product type, and may range from 1% to 50%. A typical commission rate would be 10% to 25%. For our market, gifts, the commission rate is usually 15% of the selling price, but can vary with discounting.

Security forms: Records that help the government and shipper know who you are and how to reach you.

Seller's insurance: Protects you in case clients don't pay. This can be expensive, but if you are selling large orders to potentially risky clients, it can be worthwhile.

Shipper's letter of instructions: Document that lets a shipper of a particular order know what is being shipped, the value, and how it is to be handled.

Show room: A place where a rep group or company puts its product offerings on display. Show rooms are often located within a larger building housing many different groups.

Social media: Refers to the content created by people using highly accessible and scalable publishing technologies that is intended to facilitate communications, influence and interaction with peers and with public audiences, typically via the Internet and mobile communications networks.

Social networking: Connecting with other people through Internet services. Focuses on building online communities of people who share interests and/or activities, or who are interested in exploring the interests and activities of others. Most social network services are web-based and provide a variety of ways for users to interact, such as e-mail and instant messaging services. Social networking has created new ways to communicate and share information and is being used regularly by millions of people. It currently appears that social networking will become a part of everyday life. Since social networking is a great way to let a niche or large population know about something, it often serves as a means of viral marketing. Examples: Facebook and LinkedIn.

Theory of multiple intelligences: Developed by Howard Gardner, a theory that individuals, especially children, learn in different ways and that information should be presented in many ways in order to make knowledge accessible to people with different learning and thinking styles.

Thunder Tube™: An inexpensive, hand-held sound effects device originally known as the Spring Drum, developed and manufactured by Remo, Inc., then re-created and re-positioned by Robert Fishbone.

Trade show, trade fair or expo: An exhibition organized to enable companies in a specific industry to showcase and demonstrate their latest products and services, study activities of rivals, and examine recent trends and opportunities.

Trading Partner: A person or company who can facilitate the sourcing, manufacture and transportation of goods, usually in another country. They normally do not own any means of production themselves.

Trophy Music Company: The distributors for my line of novelty percussion instruments: Thunder Tubes™, Washboard Ties™ and Bead Brain™ skull shakers. www.grotro.com

T/T: Bank wire transfer. A way to electronically move funds from one bank to another, domestically or internationally.

Twitter: A social networking and micro-blogging service. It enables its users to send and read other users' updates (known as tweets), which are text-based posts of up to 140 characters in length. Updates are displayed on the user's profile page and delivered to other users who have signed up to receive them. The service has given people the ability to do instant surveys, but there are others who think it is just ridiculous.

User Generated Commerce: The practice whereby online users contribute their content to the Internet as a form of personal ecommerce. First invented by Café Presse in 1999. Example: an individual uploads designs to Café Presse, where anyone else can buy those designs printed onto any number of products stocked by Café Press such as t-shirts, mugs, aprons, calendars, magnets and more. The designer then gets a royalty.

Venture capital: Private equity capital typically provided to early-stage, high-potential, growth companies in the interest of generating a return through an eventual realization event such as an IPO or trade sale of the company. Venture capital investments are generally made as cash in exchange for shares in the invested company. Venture capital typically comes from institutional investors and high net worth individuals and is pooled together by dedicated investment firms.

Viral marketing and viral advertising: Marketing techniques that use pre-existing social networks to produce increases in brand awareness or to achieve other marketing objectives, such as product sales. Viral promotions may take the form of video clips, interactive Flash games, adver-games, ebooks, brandable software, images, text messages, or even hard-copy print, TV, radio or word of mouth. Viral marketing/advertising can seem like the message takes on a life of its own, much like the spread of a disease, hence the term viral.

Virtual web business: A venture run entirely on the web, with no brick and mortar operations. All you'll need is a web connection, like a lap top or even a smart phone.

Voluntary Lawyers and Accountants for the Arts: Professionals who donate their services, usually through local arts agencies.

Wikipedia: A multilingual, web-based, free-content encyclopedia project, written by volunteers from around the world. Anyone can edit it, though the edits are subject to further review and substantiation. Wikipedia constantly evolves.

World wide licensing agreement: Document granting the licensee certain rights to reproduce and make use of an artist's work. Usually a licensing agreement will specify a smaller territory than the entire world. The uniqueness of our *Scream* line helped us get a world-wide license.

"You Store It" facility: A public facility in which you can store pretty much whatever you want as long as it isn't illegal or dangerous. A great place to keep excess inventory, especially if you work out of your home.